HKAC

The River in the Sky

ALSO BY CLIVE JAMES

AUTOBIOGRAPHY
Unreliable Memoirs   Falling Towards England
May Week Was In June   North Face of Soho
The Blaze of Obscurity

FICTION
Brilliant Creatures   The Remake
Brrm! Brrm!   The Silver Castle

VERSE
Other Passports: Poems 1958–1985
The Book of My Enemy: Collected Verse 1958–2003
Opal Sunset: Selected Poems 1958–2008
Angels Over Elsinore: Collected Verse 2003–2008
Nefertiti in the Flak Tower   Sentenced to Life
Collected Poems 1958–2015   Gate of Lilacs   Injury Time

TRANSLATION
The Divine Comedy

CRITICISM
The Metropolitan Critic (new edition, 1994)
Visions Before Midnight   The Crystal Bucket
First Reactions (US)   *From the Land of Shadows*
Glued to the Box   Snakecharmers in Texas
The Dreaming Swimmer   Fame in the 20th Century
On Television   Even As We Speak   Reliable Essays
As of This Writing (US)   *The Meaning of Recognition*
Cultural Amnesia   The Revolt of the Pendulum
A Point of View   Poetry Notebook
Latest Readings   Play All

TRAVEL
Flying Visits

CLIVE JAMES

The River in the Sky

A Poem

LIVERIGHT PUBLISHING CORPORATION
A Division of W. W. Norton & Company
Independent Publishers Since 1923
New York • London

Manufacturing by Versa Press
Production manager: Anna Oler

ISBN 978-1-63149-473-4

Liveright Publishing Corporation
500 Fifth Avenue, New York, N.Y. 10110
www.wwnorton.com

W. W. Norton & Company Ltd.
15 Carlisle Street, London W1D 3BS

1 2 3 4 5 6 7 8 9 0

For Prue

All is not lost, despite the quietness
That comes like nightfall now as the last strength
Ebbs from my limbs, and feebleness of breath
Makes even focusing my eyes a task –
As when, before the merciful excision
Of my mist-generating cataracts,
The money-spiders dwindled in their webs
Between one iron spandrel and the next
On my flagstone verandah, each frail web
The intermittent image of a disc
That glittered like the Facel Vega's wheel
Still spinning when Camus gave up his life,
Out past the journey's edge. Just such a dish,
Set off with dew-drops like pin-points of chrome,
Monopolises my attention here
In Cambridge as I sit wrapped in the quiet,
Stock still and planning my last strategies
For how I will employ these closing hours.
But no complaints. Simply because enforced,
This pause is valuable. Few people read
Poetry any more but I still wish
To write its seedlings down, if only for the lull
Of gathering: no less a harvest season
For being the last time. The same frail wheel
Could decorate my father's clean white headstone
In the cemetery at Sai Wan Bay, Hong Kong:
One of my gateways to the infinite
First built when I was just a little child

And flew a silver Spitfire through the flowers –
Clumps of nasturtiums sopping with their perfume –
As if they were low-lying, coloured clouds
There in Jannali, in the summer heat.
Now, one last time, my fragile treasures link
Together in review.

In ancient days
Men in my job prepared for endless travel
Across the sea of stars, where Pharaoh sailed
To immortality, but now we know
This is no journey. A long, aching pause
Is all the voyage there will ever be.
Already it is not like life. I shan't
Caress the heterae of Naukrates,
Only their images: paint on a wall,
Not vivid like a bowl of porphyry,
But pale, chipped, always fading. Here forgive me
When you come kindly visiting, as both
Our daughters do, for you three built the start
Of this tomb when you helped me weed my books
And then arrange the ones left, walls of colour
The sunlight will titrate from spring to autumn.
Rich shelves of them, these lustrous codices,
Are the first walls I see now in the morning
After the trek downstairs, though when I walk
On further, painfully, I see much more –
Boats in the windows, treasures on the terrace,
As if I weren't just Pharaoh's tomb designer
But the living god in the departure lounge
Surrounded by his glistering aftermath –

Yet everything began in these few thousand
Pages of print and plates. Books are the anchors
Left by the ships that rot away. The mud
The anchors lie in is one's recollection
Of what life was, and never, late or soon,
Will be again.

Plugged into YouTube's vast cosmopolis,
We are in Sweden, and Bill Evans plays
"'Round Midnight", Monk's most elemental thing:
Most beautiful and most bewildering
Because it builds a framework out of freedom.
At the Cambridge Union once, I watched Monk play
That song in his sharp hat and limp goatee
As if the fact that he himself composed it
Back in the day
Merely ensured he would forget it slowly,
Instead of straight away, like where he was.
His eyeballs like hot coals, he jabbed and growled,
At one stage failing to locate the keyboard
Completely. But I walked to the Blue Boar
Beside Tom Weiskel to pay awe-struck homage.
Monk thought we were the cops. He disappeared.

Only a few years later, Weiskel too
Went missing. Back in the States, majestic
In his tenure, he was skating with his daughter
On a frozen lake. She went through the thin ice
And he died diving for her. So now I
Am the only one of those three men alive.
Let's call it four. George Russell loved that number.

He heard the sparseness in the classic tones,
Though his idea of swing was Hindemith.
My future wife and I would bring him discs
That he had never heard, and he for us
Would spin the classic stuff we ought to hear.
So much of receptivity is instinct,
A lust for finding form in the unknown,
The pathway around midnight, searched by touch
When you are lost.

In Vienna once, the Princess Antoinette
Hohenlohe, most commonly called Nettie,
Showed me her family's fabulous collection
Of Degas pastels. In a chest of drawers
They were arranged in sheaves. The ballerinas
I had first seen in my Skira book in Sydney
Were all there, the colours sumptuous
Past anything that I could have imagined.
The state will get them all eventually.
A good thing, but at least they've been looked after,
Like the Klimts and Schieles in the Belvedere.
Bombarded by the photons pouring upwards,
Eventually I had to plead exhaustion.
My eyes were weary from the burning colours,
Especially the blue I never found
Again until the year I filmed in Cairo
And saw it as an inlay in pure gold –
The sky-lit death mask of Tutankhamun.

This is the way my memories connect
Now that they have no pattern.

All I can do is make the pictures click
As I go sailing on the stream of thought
Feeding the lake across which the sun strikes
To fill my sail, and every river bank
Or beach between the dunes and the sand bar
Leads to another place which I once knew,
And now, at night, can see again
In sharper outline, shadows in the shadows:
Veils, sheets and tents of coruscation
Peeling and coalescing as I travel
As if, instead of walking by the river
I were whispering across the Nullarbor
In the cockpit of the car whose silver shell
Was made of photo cells. The Sun Racer?
The Sun Voyager. Gliding is what I do,
Here at the finish, in the final hour.
It will be this way between the star clusters,
In the gulf between the galaxies.

In sunken cities of the memory
Mud-brick, dissolved in time,
Leaves nothing but the carved, cut stones
And scraps of the ceramics.
Time, it is thereby proven, is the sea
Whose artefacts are joined by separateness.

Oasis of Siwa, I call you back
Through the gilded wood of Osiris
With his inlaid eyes.
Time passes and turns black
But only in between the gold, the jewels:

Where nothing of its decoration lingers
The wood is a dark night

Sky gods appear as falcons:
Horus, the divine, is one of them.
After Rembrandt lost his wealth
He could still paint the frothed and combed
Delicacy of light on gold,
The texture of gathering darkness
Made manifest by the gleam
That it contains and somehow seems to flaunt
While dialling down. An understated festival,
His energy came back to him through memory
As mine does here and now, as if lent power
By the force of its own fading.

The slick smooth sandstone of the water stair
Lifted through space from Clifton Gardens
In Sydney where I picnicked with my mother
With all the other widows and war orphans
To the delta of the Nile
Echoes a fresco's surface, petrified.
That figure with its finger in its mouth
Is meant to be a child

Even when dancing in the caves
Of the Kimberleys
All painted adults seem serene –
The Dreamtime Dancers.
Only the children suck their fingers
As they look towards you

Waiting for their turn
At life, the long plunge into doubt

On TV at night, direct from Rio,
Olympic divers are hydraulic drills
When they go in and flatten out
To lie above the bottom of the pool
On palettes of specific bubbles

At Rio, Ren Qian, plaiting her silk thread
Of falling and revolving light
Through thirty feet of air
Goes in without a ripple.
Seen from inside the pool, her impact
Is a shout rewritten as a whisper,
A bomb exploding inwards

At Ramsgate Baths on Botany Bay
I waited half an hour
For the girl in the blue Speedo
To do her simple dive
From a mere three metres
The dive was one step up
From a peanut roll

But Ren Qian now
Spearing through my screen
Like a goddess reaching Earth
Is only a touch more beautiful
Than what I can remember
Of a human girl whose face

I have spent my life forgetting.
If you want to see a better joke
Than young desire
Just look at an old man
First gambling without chips
And then without a single steady picture
Of the silver ball

Roulette wheels in Las Vegas,
The B24's propellers
Churning sunlight on Okinawa
For the flight meant to bring
My father home
Are like collars of the priests
Heads threaded through the sun's disc
Or that tambourine the moon

At the destruction horizon
The last wall of the temple
Crashes into the water
And, pulled apart, a fresco turns to dust:
A cup of coffee gone back to the bag
Of beans by the long route,
An aeon reassigned
To form the towpath now
Of the river of my memory

This is a river song,
Linking the vivid foci
Where once my mind was formed
That now must fall apart:

A global network blasted
To ruins by the pressure
Of its lust to grow, which proves now
At long last, after all this time,
To be its urge to die.

Regard the crown of Hallas:
Cow horns, sun disc, feathers,
The centuries subtract its properties
Until you reach a Borgia Pope
The Prince of the carnival in Rio
– "I've come to help you carry
The Sun, Orpheus" –
The floats of Melbourne's Moomba festival,
Precursor of the Sydney Mardi Gras
When my first queer friends came out
To teach me music

And thus it was, because I so adored
A female singer in *The Fairy Queen*
Who sent pellucid phrases of Purcell
Into the Great Hall's vault,
That I bought from the producer
My set of *Mahagonny*
And fell for Lotte Lenya
Thousands of miles away
From where the Nazis would have liked
To lock her up and kill her

Later I learned that in America
She said the piercingly true thing

Reserved for women only:
"What was Brecht
Without Weill?"
World-wide, a million far-left male highbrows
Fainted in their tracks
At the mere suggestion Brecht might not have been
The universal sage
With lyricism as his second gun
Tucked in the armpit of the blue silk shirts
He ordered so he might look like a worker.
As phony as a two-bob watch,
Brecht was an utter bastard to his women
But Lenya had his number
And, like her character that fought James Bond,
Knives in her sensible shoes.

But this was in the future. In the past
The Naos of the Decades
From the Nile's eastern delta
Journeyed slowly to the west
Shattering all the way.
Two thousand years later
The pieces join up again
As now my soul does
Lying here so ill my memories –
Which, you will have noticed,
Are stoked with countless deaths –
Could fuel a nebula

For my nets of recollection shine
Like the tree-tops of Kokoda

Late at night
The phosphorescent outlines
Assemble, interpenetrate
Where our fathers and our uncles
Looked up into the ceiling
Of silver gods –
Imagine Michelangelo
Confined to chrome and diamonds –
And wondered where the enemy
Lay cradling his guns
In the darkness of the jungle floor

On the far side of the world
Above that sea of lights
Translated into flak
And burning blast-points
The Aussie Mosquito flyers
Went in silhouette
Across the Ruhr
And when the war was over
There was one of them I saw
Bowl fast balls at the SCG
Against the greatest team
The West Indians ever sent.
When I tell Australians now
That I saw Keith Miller play
They realise how old I am:
Like being there for Troy,
Like having seen
The flare-path for great Hector
Guiding him home

And the whirlpools
Of the Merlins in the English dark.

And in Adelaide I met
That other blessed flyer,
Kym Bonython himself
The squatter who had everything –
The galleries of paintings,
The properties the size
Of Luxembourg, the wives
Out of a classic fable – the only
Connoisseur at his exalted level
To have driven in a demolition derby.

When Eurilla, his great house, burned to the ground
The flames took paintings by Arthur Boyd,
By Nolan, Olsen, Lloyd Rees and Brett Whiteley
Five thousand jazz discs, many of them signed
(Duke Ellington was his house-guest several times)
And all his books. It must have seemed the wrath
Of God, yet Kym came back
As full of joy as always.
There was a lesson there
And I still don't know what it is.
You have to be that way
And, above all, stick to your real speed,
Which was, for him, the way the perspex windscreen
Of the Mossie ate the miles.
It was the tempo of his life,
Visible again in how he decked

The grille tray of his Bristol 403
With a set of bullock horns.

But pause now, for the richness
The Australians so seldom know
That they are heirs to:
For ours is a land of legends
That seldom recognise
Each other's names.
It isn't history that we lack
It is the habit
Of thinking in it.
Do you think the Chappel Brothers
Thrilled to the name of Florey
Who gave us penicillin?

As a student in Sydney
I knew the nurse that held,
While the West Indians were touring,
The specific job of counting
The illegitimate children
Of Wesley Hall,
And even the most prejudiced
Of our home-grown male fuckwits
Knew it had to be
The privilege of a visiting divinity
To sow his seed across the map
Like splashes of a star-field.

Barracking on the Hill
At the SCG

Some genius timed his question
Exactly right as Hall
Strode back for his endless run:
"You going home, Wesley?"

I should have guessed right then
It's a sufficient destiny
To make the right remark
At exactly the right time:
A poem might be more than that
But it is never less.

Jackal-headed, carrying the *ankh*
Like a designer handbag,
Seth drowns Osiris
Whose wife, Isis, finding him at last,
– Isis, great in magic –
Restores his life.

Do that for me when you come back
From Kashmir, the high country
And bend to me as my best teacher did
In Jannali infants' school,
Awarding me, for getting something right,
First Choice of Blocks

As this chap strictly didn't:
Osiris *vegetans* the corn mummy.
Black wood-pulp case and falcon head of gold

To set off the blue hair of lapis
Chic as Louise Brooks.
Green skin, king of the underworld
What's not to worship?

All is not lost, Adrastus, though thy name
Might make it seem so.
In a long frieze there are youngsters of the time
Preserved in rock,
The very way the youthful Randall Jarrell
Is Ganymede in Nashville's Parthenon
Or the Winged Venus on the US dime
Is the wife of Wallace Stevens

The names of creatures can mislead.
From any sky, the cry most heavenly
Is of the butcher bird
Whose name is full of sharp-edged death
Evoking as it does the heavy-bladed
Cleaver of Halley,
The butcher in Jannali
Who was named after a comet.

Bluey, his cattle dog that bit me,
Was taken to be destroyed
As soon now I will be, I who have heard
The butcher bird sing in the valley,
The gulley that ran through Heathcote,
Where I swam in the pint-sized tributary
Of Cook's river

Down through the translucence,
And the fleeing convicts hid in caves,
Planning their walk to China

Born in the annotated district
Where Cook's two science boffins
Banks and Solander
Named all the life they saw,
– One imagines the wallabies
Bunking off,
Spooked by the spectacle
Of bipeds in white wigs –
I should have been more careful
To remember everything

But say this of the butcher bird:
Both sexes sing
A high-pitched, complicated melody.
Think of Netrebko and Garanča
Unspooling their divine duet in *Lakme*,
– They're there on YouTube,
An electronic hall of apparitions
All put together in the final years
Of a single century
Since the Wright Brothers took off –
And remember the whip-birds of Avalon
Lashing the sky's back like a criminal
All along the valley

My Americans in Cambridge
Had names from comic books:

Star Lawrence, Mike Smith, Pete Mazan
Steve Greenblatt, Myron Magnet and Tom Weiskel

The skis were long in those days
And Mike Smith's, made of steel,
Would clatter on the moguls
Of Zürs am Arlberg
As he straight-lined a whole hill.
None of them liked the war
But you couldn't see them losing

Back teaching in the States,
Weiskel, to save his daughter,
Didn't stop to take his skates off
Before he went in to find her
And they both died in the cold

He'd understand, if ever I should see him
In the halls of Dis,
I just about put up with the idea
Of his death, but not hers.
But he won't need telling that,
Today, in this long winter
When I shout at my two daughters
That I cannot see them in the dark
– For Christ's sake wear your arm-bands –
I threaten them with my own death
Through fear, and not with theirs
Of which they have such small conception
They still dress, after nightfall,
Like commandos from a rubber boat

On a secret mission
To murder me with guilt

But even while he moaned and groaned
Monk couldn't blur
The structure of a tune carved out of fog
Because it is a blur already,
Like a mist by Turner full of different
Thicknesses of rain. Back in the fifties
I used to play the Monk Blue Note LPs
To my future wife. She still
Has them on her shelves today
Along with all the dirt-cheap Turnabouts
Of Brendel's first, best cycle
Of the Beethoven sonatas
And the Supremes albums
Star Lawrence gave us: Baby, Baby
Where did our love go?
Ira shaimase
I go and I come back

We have been married now so long
Vinyl is back in fashion.
As if burning cakes of peat
Were once again the chic
Way of making fire

If my ashes end up in an hour-glass
I can go on working.
Patterns of gravity
Will look like writing.

Remember me, sings Dido,
But ah! Forget my fate

Wind shapes the dunes
Above which swallows stream
To Europe, with a pit-stop at Gibraltar
Reminding them that Africa was soft
With sliding surfaces of singing sand.
The whole world, if you wait long enough
Is full of falling.

The *clavadista* checks the tower
On the cliffs from which he dives
Turning two thirds of the way down
To mark the point
Where all the somersaults are over
And he must go in feet first or else break

A sleep so deep I woke instead of dying
To a dark evening where the household diodes
Were pearls and emeralds
Shining like tiny gods
Or atomic insects
Networks of linked pin-points
Like the floor-plan of the Tuileries
Marked out by Philibert de l'Orme
Or Galileo's drawings of the moon

In the ancient Tuileries
Before it burned
Was the upstairs little room
Of the lovely young Hélène

And the staircase that Ronsard
Climbed like a leopard dying
To reach her and recite
His poems to her face
Au soir, à la chandelle.

So that now her loveliness
Is repeated in the world
On a million paper pages
As if, in the glass rapids
Of the Versailles Mirror Hall,
Its multiplicity
Disintegrates forever
And floods down the hard steps
To the theatre in the stairs
Of frigid Pompadour

Those stairs I climb each evening
Before a night of walking
The paths and park parades
Of my lost, networked world,
And as I climb I see
A troubled shade go past me
So keen to leave the earth
He has air under his heels.

"So let death have me, then,"
I hear Primo Levi say
"If it wants me so much."
And one night or another
As I journey to my bed

I see his ghost fall past me
And I give thanks for my life,
Though that long life began
When my father was a slave
And suffered every day
In faraway Japan

But he saved my future for me
Though it began in turmoil
And the bitter, aching cries
Of my dear, stricken mother
– *Unhappy Queen! Then is the common breath*
Of rumour true, in your reported death
And I, alas, the cause! – So Dryden speaks
For Virgil, and I hear it: my first death,
But some sense of a beauty absolute
And undisturbed
Has haunted my life always
Ever since a lovely apparition
Took my father to the underworld –
Always I see Karsavina
Crossing the stage in Paris
Failing to find him,
She not having realised yet
He has turned into the Firebird –
I have known and moved
To the rhythm of incipient oblivion
My every poem, every song, a requiem.

High peaks of Morocco
Snow stained pink by grains of the Sahara sand

The wind brings, and the crystals form around
Like a crust of icing sugar

Nifty as a bobcat
The stooping falcon
Folds and goes down
High in the Himalayas
Snow leopards dive
To the next cliff-face
Where the ibexes find footholds
The size of coins

As you first see, outlined against the clouds,
The Gansu prancing horse
With one foot on the flying swallow
And you fly too:
Bronze of the Eastern Han
Celestial steed

Breezeways in the Summer Palace
Are bright to look at as the radiant tails
Of peacocks by Whistler
The extra layer of luxuriance
That being painted puts on

After all of Whistler's travels and his exiles
The Peacock Room is in America.
The Amber Room that so belonged to Russia
Is nowhere that we know
But what is lost the mind replaces:
That perfect small Matisse
In Melbourne, nesting

In a single room donated
By a family who, in exile safe at last,
Could long for Europe without penalty
Goodnight Vienna

So far to come, through so much night to flee,
And they graced my life
Not just with the spectacle of perfect
Carpentry, but with the lavish
Spareness of Matisse's colours
Fitting like an airy jigsaw
In a wooden frame
As now I watch my elder daughter
In all of her designs
Pick out the places

Where the air will do the work
A spell from the lavishness
Whose lush too-muchness kills,

It's not that the pre-Raphaelites
Weighed in with too much colour
In my view, but that they
Gave us no rest from it

And Hokusai knew how to rest
Even when he painted
A roaring surf
Like the one I watched at Curl Curl
Going crazy for two days

When, in the mornings now,
She stops off in my studio to make
My cup of super coffee
She parks her launch-code bag
Which has the secrets in it
Of pastel panels and of air-rinsed cloth
Before she walks across the park
To where the only half-filled frame
Awaits her touch

In the studio my wife approved
Indeed, made possible,
In this bright twilight of our lives
This incandescent darkening

And my younger daughter too
Is here each Saturday
To help me watch *The West Wing*
For the second time.
We like it best when Donna
Unpicks the moral problem:
We like Abby not so much.
Too fond of spreading gloom.
We should be glad to see her,

But in Stockard Channing's downturned
Beady grimaces
There is too small a vestige
Of how, in *The Big Bus*,
Her Ida Lupino spoof
Lit up the desert

As you, on any Sunday
While the clear light or the clouded
Illuminates these books,
Are here to spin the disc
That so late in our lives
Brings us back to the Italians.
Right now it's *Manon Lescaut*
Conducted by Sinopoli
At a time when both Domingo
And Mirella Freni
Were in their clearest voice
And we might trace the both of them
Back through their brilliant years
But the trouble with this method
Of romping through the archives
Is already showing up.
Anything entirely lovely
We want to hear again next week
And life might simply fail to be that long
Even for you
While me we know about
And the Russians are here too
To remind us of our Moscow
Where we sat through, in the Kremlin,
An entire folk dance evening
While hungering specifically
For Tchaikovsky and Moussorgsky

But they were waiting for us here:
Marina and the false Czarevitch
In their sublime duet

From that ancient boxed-set *Boris*
That still smells of cheap glue
Just might be singing me to death
Krasavitsa moya
Aha me proud beauty

So that stuff you love in *Parsifal*
We'd better get back to pronto
Remembering that this week
While you're at Covent Garden
I'll be with the high divers
In Rio de Janeiro
And the length of life
Is much less like that lovely
Good Friday Music
Than falling from the tower.

River in the Sky
River of January
Your beauty still destroys me, Rio.
I watch you as I falter
Hearing the whisper of farewell
From the beach at Ipanema

Where Mariana de Moraes
Cross-legged on the sand
In her microdot bikini
Sweetly reincarnated
The original appeal
That her grandmother once had
For the poet Vinicius,

And the purple star-bursts
Where, in the forest of Petropolis,
The *quaresmas* bloom.

Walls of reliefs, floors of reliefs
In Dante's Purgatory as the road climbs
So like the staircase up to San Miniato
Are united by a concept
Of redemption judiciously postponed.
You will come to a time
When everything you touch
Is made one in just that way
But with a plethora of shadings:
Imagine the last aria of *Otello*
Backed by the fourteen-voice climactic *tutti*
Of *Il Viaggio a Reims*
When they all burst into collective coloured fire,
A syncopated *feu de joie* for voices

In the time that I first knew you
Not knowing you would be my wife
Just a few years in the future,
The deal must have been settled
On the day, back there in Sydney,
When we listened to Callas
And the others in the sextet
Of *Lucia di Lammermoor*
Over and over:
It's a sure sign
When you launch yourselves at beauty
As if, carved from one diamond,

It can't possibly wear out,
As if you could eat the stuff.

Conducting the sweet uproar
Of that divine sextet
For the first time in post-war Berlin
Das Wunder Karajan
Ordered another encore
To stop the riot.
Play it again, Sam.
This was the beginning of the world
As the sun rays climbed
From the rim of the Pacific
The pillars of your portico
And yours too, Adrastus

You see, I remember you are here
Beside me, though your chair
Is in the shadows
To guard my last trajectory
Into the final silence
Which is what this is, even though the gold
Still gleams,
As if it could be heard
Like the children in the park
On their brand-new bicycles.
Where the idling click
Of the Sturmey-Archer gears
In the hubs of their back wheels
Recalls with such precision
The chirrup of the insects

In the Gardens of Boboli
Back there when we had barely
Finished being young

The orpiment degrades
In sycamore-fig pegs and dowels,
The once-bright lemon-yellow feather
Further fades:
Birds at the corners of a coffin set
Will lose the definition
Their coded colours gave them.
Now look at your hands,
Remembering what Rilke said:
How he had held
His father's fading daguerreotype
In hands that were fading too.

A temple lasts but houses will dissolve
And the temple, also,
Is eaten by the sea.
Even the monuments on land
Upstream and far into the desert
Drown in the dry air.
At Abu Simbel, back when time began
Greek men from Rhodes
Had scratched their names on the colossal
Statue of Rameses:

Kilroy was here.
It was what the young Marines
Would paint on a smashed amphtrac

On the beach at Tarawa
And we read it in Australia
Like a message from the future.
When the Super Constellation
Came in to land at Mascot
Throwing its long curved shadow,
And I was there
Sprawled in the dunes beside my bike,
The same hide that I chose
To watch the Stratocruiser
Completing its last leg from far Hawaii
Tilt in the final curve
Of its approach
And send a flashing signal
That reached back to the sun.

The compound Pratt and Whitney
Engines of the American
Trans-Pacific heavies
Would rattle the Cooper Louvres
Of our back verandah
While my mother served the junket
Which I watched tremble
As if the Earth were being born
In the long blast of an explosion
Right there among the towers
Of the landing lights.

Thank God and every other god there is
That time is an aesthete
Who strips the colours from the Parthenon.

We are left, were it not
For the play of shadow,
With the acres and square miles
Of Fuseli's white ghost-flesh
But it beats the polychromatic
Crap out of the Disneyland
That antiquity once was.

This is the upside of the great fading:
Without the paint to spoil the alabaster
The Cypriot nude youth looks truly suave,
Smooth as the swan that pilots the slow sun
Along with the deceased, soon to be me,
Across the waters of the underworld:
The sea like sky, the sky like sea
Life like a puff of sand
Kicked from the shallows

And I saw it first at Tuggerah
That puff of sand,
The shallows of Lake's Entrance
Illuminated by
The path of water-lights,
And then again at Viareggio
When it was coming on to evening
And again in Biarritz
In the paddle-pool lagoon
Near the steps up from the beach
Where the tots would dig their tunnels
To the halls of the eternal
Though they went down to no darkness

In the volatile wet sand
But only blinked their eyes against the sun.

In Browning's song about the Bishop's tomb
Peach-blossom marble
Has the lustre of a name so new to us
It's as if we've been given it to suck.
Once, that was true for all of Egypt.
The whole deal was a knickerbocker-glory
Popsicle, and all that you see now
Fades to fit in with your forthcoming
Dying breath,

The musical approach
So halting, intermittent,
Of the ice-cream man in summer

The last gasp that sounds so much like wonder
Stunned by human beauty
As once we thought to die
From a single photograph of Ava Gardner
In *Pix* or *Women's Weekly*
Or felt the cosmos tremble
When, early in *Rear Window*,
Grace Kelly first came fluttering into vision
Across the room which until then
Was strictly finite.

Suavely wolfing down the open slather
Of being the only non-gay female
In the entire area

Patrick Leigh-Fermor's first exotic mistress,
The Princess Michel Cantacuzène Speranski,
Parked her shapely bottom on the bumper
Of her vast Hispano-Suiza:
Chariots for eternity
Make every tomb a multi-car garage.

I met the great adventurer only once –
Met him well, and not by moonlight –
And straightaway could see his love for women
Depended on the need to be forgiven
The tight-lipped histrionics
Of his winning ways
That worked in every language.
For him it was too easy:
He was hard-wired for seduction
Till he was nearly ninety.
Charm is a worm-hole to Andromeda

In the church-rich stretch of river bank
That runs from Krems to Melk
He made out of the Danube
His stately watergate
Into the East
– *Vide* his perfect paragraphs,
Each one a baroque stanza,
In his book *A Time of Gifts* –
And ages later
When I, too, walked that route
I found, in the skyscraping
Krupp castle of Blünbach

That even when my hostess
Wore her leaf-green *Jagdkostum*
To indicate her informality
There was a certain strain
Perhaps because I was her only guest
And she and I
Were backed up by a servant each,
Each servant trembling
In the starting blocks like Hector Hogan
Running for Australia in Helsinki.

This was the Europe Napoleon had need of,
Whose Europe included Egypt.
The pyramids were built for him
To use as cufflinks.
Power though, or even wealth
Might not mean beauty.
A dancer in her lovely flight
Cannot be bought or even built
She is, as Whitman said
– Whose dancing at the end consisted
Of capering in a shallow pond –
Embalmed with love in this twilight song
Though some would say that he was really
Thinking of Lincoln in long underwear.
(Always important to remember
That Whitman, though he made his gestures
Towards the multivalence
Of sexual desire,
Was a lot more queer
Than any coot.)

As you should with any art
You must love him at the very outer edge
Of your own proclivities.

I always travelled better
When I was not a guest
And owed no one a favour.
On a flagstone forecourt set into the lawn
That later swept down to the river Plate
From that grand house on the coruscating hill
The first year I went back to Buenos Aires,
The tango dancers gathered in the dusk
And as the night came on, the burning lamps
Killed insects while the dancers brought to life
The spirit of their lovely craft. I, too,
Was blessed that night, the merest interloper
Among the home-grown adepts, but when I
Was told that the most delicately gracious
Of all the dancing ladies was stone blind –
You need to know that she danced like a dream
And I had watched her until my eyes ached –
For once I got my courage out of hock
At the right time, and I asked her to dance
Careful to tell her that I looked like Errol Flynn,
So she need not fear she was ill-matched.

She'd hardly heard of him but still she laughed
And as the opening chords of "Caminito"
Reached out into the night, she reached for me,
And straight away I was in charge of her
As if my task were steering a sweet cloud

Through halls of air. Although, in her high heels
With lacquered straps she was as tall as I
Almost exactly, she made up for that:
She warmed my shoulder with her tilted cheek.
The night was warm already. Now it burned,
As if the way ahead were carved by starlight.
A time to remember, as I breathed her perfume,
That the tango began as a parade at court
Before it was plunged by history
Into the squalor of the dives and docks.
I even dared to steer her through a *puente*
That laid her out as if embracing sleep
On a couch of night under the silver stars.
If you're a dancer too you'll know too well
To make her lean that much is the best chance
To drop the woman even if she can see,
But this one gave me all her confidence:
Gave me her life, in fact. Beyond that night –
Beyond, indeed, the third dance of our *tanda* –
I saw her never once again, not even
In a fevered dream; but the very fact that she
Had never once seen anything stayed with me,
And is with me now, as now she is with you,
My young male readers, poets of the future
As I sort my books and grammars
!Quién sabe, si supieras
que nunca te he olvidado . . . !
For the long flight back to England

And waiting for me there
At the far end of the river in the sky

Would be the river caves
For as if my fate were sealed
I had begun to dream
Of how my life might end

Only a month before my health broke down,
I sat at Rossini's on the Quay
Where Sydney is at its most magnetic,
And I wrote of the blind girl in Buenos Aires,
That other mighty dreamland on the water.
The ferries growled and piped. On foot below
The shedding jacarandas, gulls patrolled
Like condescending white supremacists
Sharing with pigeons the enhanced green lawn,
The purple passage that announces spring
In Sydney, our October tapestry
Flown in for two weeks from a Loire chateau.
Sitting to write, as I had often done
For years then, at Rossini's on the Quay –
The outside tables don't catch too much sun
Late in the day – I looked across the harbour
To Luna Park where it nestles at the foot
Of the Bridge's north-west pylon on the lip
Of Lavender Bay, the very name a joke,
For there the reeking prison hulks were anchored
In the colony's first years. The Park was built
Before my birth. My mother took me there
When the war was not yet over, and I saw
Soldiers dive down the hill-high slippery dips
In the hall called Coney Island – no one knew
The name was a cheap import – heavy-booted

Surfers in uniform on wooden combers
In flight above the bumps, gripping their thin
Slick mats, harbingers of the boogie-board.
Young couples, queuing for the River Caves,
Nuzzled each other's faces. Why was that?
Vaguely I guessed that the whole adult world
Must feel far different to the people in it,
Even in here, where they behaved like children.

Like children, adults on the Tumblebug
Would sick their Fairy-Floss. A flood of noise
Ran south out of the bay into the city
Except on Sunday evening. Silent then,
The Park drew breath for one more shouting week,
A rhythm it maintained until the winter,
When it shut down. But winter was very short.
In spring it opened up again, as loud
As a painted silk tie from America
With a fat knot. Local residents wore ear-plugs,
Held meetings and wrote letters to the *Herald*.
Men in white coats took some of them away.

So it roared on until the year I left:
Before the old Big Dipper was torn down
You could hear the shrieks of girls across the dark,
Trapped voices from the blazing jewel-box,
Le Jardin de Plaisir with coloured gravels,
Our Vauxhall Gardens. Everyone went there
At least once in a year while they grew up
Until the Ghost Train burned. From that night on
The place was rigged for safety, shorn of thrills –

Fifteen years later, when I first came back,
The volume had been turned down to a murmur –
And rebuilt often, yet retained its face:
A plaster clown whose big mouth held the turnstiles.

Always the candy bulbs shone through the night,
But now they shone by day. I could see beams
Of colour in the sunlight. Were there prisms
Piled up like fruit, a rack of fresnel lenses?
A Technicolor *Lichtdom* stained the streaks
Of cirrus. Had they turned the place into
Some kind of laser farm? I asked the waiter
If he could see what I saw. He said no
In an Italian accent. I paid up
And caught the ferry to McMahon's Point,
The little white boat that still calls in first
(Unless they've changed the routes since I got sick)
At the wharf a short walk from the much subdued
King Jester who has done his time, not quite
Chop-fallen, still puff-cheeked, but his first flush
Of merriment a memory. The gatekeeper
Smiled not at all. She sat at a plain desk
The way she always had. Miss Coleman said:
"It's good to see you, Vivian. Such joy
Was something I did not always feel when you
Arrived at school on those days that you deigned
To turn up, often clinging to the hem
Of your mother's skirt." School was a weatherboard
One-room affair in the bush behind Jannali,
The suburb on the Illawarra line
We lived in all the War. She ruled her shed

With kindly strictness, but the noun was what
I felt more than the adjective. "And yet,"
She said, "When you were there, your quickness with
The words left me with no alternative
But to confer on you First Choice of Blocks.
You might have, though, shared some of your prize out
Without being told, instead of sneaking off
To use the whole set in some vast construction
The other children did not dare approach,
Fearing your spite." Her frown was back in place
So many decades on, so long beyond
Her death. She read my thoughts. "I married, gave
Up work, had two boys, both more sweet than you.
One of them died of polio. Tonight
You'll be our only visitor. Your ticket
Is the receipt from your café. You kept it?
You're coming on." Her use of my real name
Had hauled me back into her power. I wondered,
Looking around while she wrote on my bill –
A wooden pen, steel nib, white china inkwell –
Where the old turnstiles were. There was nothing there,
And no noise from inside except the *adagio*
Of the Ninth, with Toscanini in command.

You can always tell it's him. He keeps the pace:
The beauty never slows the steady march,
And always sounds more sumptuous for that.
"We call it Dream World now." She curled a lip.
"Rather commercial, but it fits the facts.
Take this note to your mother." My receipt
Now held a faultless line of copperplate.

"Young Vivian would do well, if he were here
More often." Much abashed, I now could see
She had been lovely. Lucky man, her husband.
She tipped me off that she could still read minds.
"Perhaps," she said, "and certainly I was,
Until our lives were changed by grief. But you,
I'm told, know something about that. Good luck."

And so I moved on through the arch, to walk
The empty main street lined with the attractions
I knew of old, and all of it for me.
Somebody changed the music. *Pictures at
An Exhibition*: my first piece of classical
Unless you count Caruso singing "*Vesti
la giubba*" on an HMV 78,
To which I listened like the label's dog,
Transfixed though clueless. The asphalt was bare:
Except for those behind the carts and stalls
Of the concessions, not a living soul
Was in the street. And then, as soon as I
Had noticed this, abruptly it was full,
But with no ordinary crowd. Here were
Brief images, succeeding one another,
Of all the crowds that I had ever seen
Since I had sailed to Europe and beyond.
I recognised the sampling technique
Of dreams. So that was why this place
Was now called Dream World! Knowing now
That none of this was really there, I thought
To pinch myself awake. "Wake up," the ice-cream man
Said as my double cone of Dairy Whip –

Always the greatest treat I was allowed,
Or, come to that, that I could well imagine –
Dripped on my hand and wrist. It tasted warm,
Then far too cold, then just right. It was gone,
The cone included. "You always ate too fast."
The ice-cream man, removing his white nose,
Revealed himself as another of my teachers,
Old Mr Slavin. "Watching you eat play-lunch
Convinced me your metabolism was
That of a tiger shark in short serge pants.
When any of the other boys had nose-bleeds
It was over in five minutes. Yours, three hours."
He was smiling, though. He'd done that even when
He caned me: the first man I ever noticed
Could put his words together, when he spoke,
As if they had been written. "Writing your
Reports, aware your mother would be proud,
Gave me great satisfaction. Time for you
To try the River Caves. I think you'll find
Your boat is waiting for you." Pushing through
Hundreds of people from a Cairo souk,
A Hong Kong market, a Chicago mall,
The Ginza *san-chome* crossing at high noon,
A Berlin night-club and a London Tube
Station at rush hour to the ticket booth
Of the River Caves, which seemed, from the outside,
No more than a plain hut of wooden slats
Painted a drab deep olive green, I looked
In at the window, thinking I would find
Another of my early teachers, though
I'd learned by then the most I could expect

Was the unexpected. There was no face there
To greet me, and the bright interior
Was blinding and entirely out of scale
With its surroundings. The Amalienburg
In all its glory blazed and danced as Mozart
Took over from Moussorgsky. Cuvilliés
Might just have ladled on the final scoop
Of molten silver. Mirrors multiplied
The space towards infinity. The swirls
Of plaster mouldings were a maelstrom
Of prettiness, a frail rococo heaven
Unpeopled at first glance, but then I saw
That though Cuvilliés had left the building –
I looked hard, since a dwarf could hide with ease
Behind the merest of the porcelain stoves –
There was indeed an architect. Incongruous
In his blue suit, he walked out of a mirror
And crossed the tiny vastness in three strides.

"But sometimes more is even more than less,"
Said Mies. "An interesting polarity,
This balance of two forces in your mind,
The tense aesthetic coupling which dictates
That when you think of riotous luxury –
Think of the extravagantly decorative
Whose linking arabesques provide the structure,
As they do here, or in the matching piece
To this pavilion, the petite Theatre
Of the Residenz assembled out of panels
That could be packed away until a war
Was over, or of Vierzehnheiligen,

The Church of Fourteen Saints, or the bright hall
In which Natasha danced – you always think
Of me, whose whole idea of wealth
Was the exact, the minimal steel strip,
The clean frame for the nothingness of glass
With all proportions candidly exposed,
A very different elegance than this.
But your perception is correct. Great pomp
Can have a clean grid, and the self-proclaimed
Simple be sometimes cluttered. For that truth
One only needs to see the fumbled work
Of my rivals in the International Style,
To make no mention of their surrogates:
Giftless if diligent, mere journeymen,
Their Avenue of the Americas
Spreading cheap drama to a tasteless world.
Your task, while you are here, will be to find
The rationale that underpins a show
Of chaos. It exists, you may be sure.
In your mind still, *De Stijl* is the ideal
As once it was in mine, a feast of the austere.
Pass me the bag." I found my hand was heavy
With a Naugahyde hold-all. I passed it through
The slit below the glass. He opened it,
Glanced in, and grunted. "Dollars. Excellent.
Never forget that I came from a time
When that much money had to go by truck.
The Nazis fixed that, but they ruined me
In every other way, although I signed
The oath of loyalty to the regime.
Much good it did me. Nowhere left to work

Except America. I respected Frank Lloyd Wright,
But Fallingwater is a builder's yard
Beside my Farnsworth House, don't you agree?"
Not staying for an answer, he stepped down
With a stout grace that recalled Fellini's father
Into an open oblong in the floor
Soon covered by a thin black slab that formed
Before my startled eyes out of thin air,
But just from its neat outline you could tell
The plan was his, austerely elegant.

Left fatherless again, I joined the queue
For boats, low-down flat punts parked nose to tail
In the dark stream stirred by the waterwheel
That once seemed so enormous. Two by two
The lovers took their seats, four pairs per punt,
Kissing and giggling. Kisses were more open
Than I remembered them, though modes of dress
Were all from when I hungered to grow up:
Skirts, twin sets, shirts with collars, no blue jeans.
I recognised some faces. Debbie Reynolds
Hugged Carleton Carpenter. *Two Weeks With Love*:
I saw it three nights running. Part of half
A dozen couples, visible six times,
Grace Kelly kissed James Stewart, Gary Cooper,
Prince Rainier, Bing Crosby, all the men
Who loved her. Ten times. There was Ingrid Bergman
With Humphrey Bogart, never real-life lovers,
But here they seemed so. Primed for a catalogue
Of couples like the one in Canto V
Of the *Inferno*, I searched further, but the theme

Changed when I blinked, and now they were all children
Progressing two by two and hand in hand
From the playground of Kogarah Infants' School
Into the room that held my class, 2B,
While suddenly Prokoviev gave the measure
Of the ball where Romeo met Juliet:
A stately minuet and then the storm,
And all brought on by just one look, one touch,
The heat of a girl's palm. I blinked again.
Church Fellowship. After the Social, when
I walked her home – she had a name, but she
Might yet breathe – and she let me put my arm
Around her waist. Later she let me stroke
Her breasts, and then the lovely warmth between
Her legs, the spill of tenderness
That Courbet thought all men must feel
Touching the cleft of birth. Her legs
Trembled so softly. The first throb of power.
The waterwheel became a blur,
The propeller of a Pratt and Whitney Twin
Wasp radial engine revving up for takeoff
From Okinawa after VJ Day
For the long flight to Australia. The blur screamed.

The blur slowed down again. I was alone.
The queue was gone, my boat was all for me,
With cushions in the front seat. I climbed in,
Stretched out, and the wooden rack below the water
Keel-hauled the boat into the shallow rapids
And through the first cave's entrance. It was dark,
But the stream was narrow, I could tell. Inches away

On either side, a field of lights began,
A darkness full of diodes, as if cats
Had tickets to the gallery, or insects
Were just before my eyes.

In the abyss
It must be like that, when the lights of fish
Or crabs or eels or worms betray no sign
Of how far off they are until your own
Light source illuminates, at just arm's length,
A bag of warts kept open by long teeth,
Some star turn in the benthic horror show,
Hideous for no reason one can see
For they don't glimpse each other from the night
Of birth through all their stygian nights
Until they die.

Here were no distances, but I could tell
That all this information would resolve
Itself to images, and I expected
That these would have to do with love, desire,
Even salacity, so stirred I'd been
By those scenes at the entrance, and yet now
There was a beach, and a procession came,
A lurching litter with my father's body
Wasted almost to nothing. It was too much
For me, that sight. I fell and slept, and woke
Alone to the cries of seagulls. There I left
The River Caves, but knew I would return
In the last years I would be well, if such there were:
This was a case

Of the death rites that confirmed my lasting vision
And many, many times till I got sick
I rode the Qantas airliners downhill
Like billycarts into the dawning city
After the long flight home.

In Sydney's pretty Strand Arcade
There was a coffee bar
Hissing with the uproar
Of Continental coffee
Manned until recent times
By Jewish ladies from Vienna
Whose complex hair-do's would,
Without the air-conditioning,
Have been impossible.

When I first saw them back in the year dot
I was too pig-ignorant to ever ask them
By what chance they had sailed to safety,
But there was no excuse for me
For being shy in later years
When I was flying in three times a year
Or more and always saw them
Before my illness locked me into Europe
And old age took them to wherever
Worn-out people go.
Well, I will find that out
For myself, and meanwhile
The coffee from this glittering machine
My elder daughter has just bought me
Is almost as sumptuous as theirs was,

Though experience suggests
That for the bean to yield its full rich tang
The mechanism needs to be backed up
By three million square miles of desert.
You need the red ochre
In the background, heaped like dust.

The deep, rich secret of the Strand Arcade
Lies not in its wrought iron or marble flooring
But in the distance from its cool boutiques
To the deep pools of the Olgas

Nothing but coincidence
That the ladies ran their shop
Only half the aisle away
From the tiny model train
– I wrote a poem for it
Which was the harbinger
Of this one now –
That ran in circles through
Its plaster landscape
A miniature reminder
That the train they never caught
Full sized and far away
Would have taken them to death.

Ages beneath Japan
In the sea-floor trench off Fuji
Distorted giant sharks
Too ghastly for a nightmare
Have expanding mouths like luggage

Twisting in the wind:
By virtue of deep cameras
And oceans of hot light
We can see them now
When once only the Hubble
Telescope could reach
Into the brilliant cloud
Before the universe's outer edge
Speeds up as if to leave us

On the wall of death
Watergate burglars in a clumsy fresco
Like the Beagle Boys
Tiptoe towards nemesis
Through the world's last junk shop
Crowded like a *brocante* in Biarritz
With stuff no longer precious

It's not the Mona Lisa that needs explaining
But the bamboo-framed firescreen
Bordered with faded fabric
Pretending to be a cast-off chunk of cloth
From some unnamed chateau
Or the case of dirt-cheap books
That were never sent for binding

On the hillsides of Petropolis
Where the *quaresmas* burn like sapphires
In the deep jade *floresta*
You will think the Douanier
Rousseau as a child

Painted the interiors
Of his tree-houses
And left them there as beacons
For the landing parties from Atrophon
Looking to prepare the site
For the home of John Travolta
So far into the future

And you and our two daughters
Built this paradise for me,
So I, though weak from illness
Like a kitten on a treadmill,
Might read and write my heart away

For this, though so carefully reassembled
Scarcely a mile from where the circus
Comes to call each year
On Midsummer Common

– Where my smaller daughter, riding on my shoulders,
Would always steer me out across the park
Towards the tumbling octopus
Growling and grunting in its shirt of lights
And take one look and once more steer me home –

Or Ashton's circus that once brought
To Kogarah, in the paddock
At the top of Sunbeam Ave,
Its three entire ponies
And the girl in the gold leotard
That was frayed and slightly scorched

From being washed too hot
Stood on her hands
Deciding not to tell me
– Or so I now deduce –
That when I turned up tomorrow
The circus would be gone
And she and I
Who had barely even kissed
Would not meet for a year
Or maybe ever

On the Barrier Reef
In the channel at Lizard Island
Chippy was a turtle
With a biscuit-sized triangle
Missing from his shell's edge
So its absence was the first
Thing about him that you noticed
As he and his friends and family
Swam in the clear shallows

In the lagoon on Lizard Island
Chippy and his friends
Swam just above the sea grass:
The formation turtles
Went flying at a speed
Related to the turning Earth
Like solitude to stillness.
How could we see so sharply
Creatures that covered distance
At a thousand miles an hour

Propelled by a mere gesture
A flipper scarcely waving
In water clear as air?

The mind in a late flowering
With its own decay for soil
Is the Rolls of the Maharaja
Of Cooch Behar
Driven slowly up and down
The short stretch of paved road
While he long ago drank gin
From a leather-covered flask
Obtained in Jermyn St,
And history did to him
And all his vast possessions
What time does to me now

The tomb for Kah and Merit was designed
By Kah himself, a leading tomb designer,
Which surely must explain why it was hard
To find. At least three thousand years went by
And it was never robbed. Today the proof
That Kah, his wife and all the gear they gathered
For the voyage out across the starry sky
Moved not an inch except from one museum
To another, is on view in Turin.
Back in the desert cliff, the painted ceiling
Is more or less intact, and charming still,
But no, there was no journey, just a custom,
Capped by this standard academic looting,
And maybe this is custom too, when I

Give credit to my gathered images
As if they might come with me,
And you, too, come with me
Just as if the afterlife
Were life itself.

But no, there is no journey,
There never was a journey,
There is just a multiform
Rearrangement and displacement
Around the epicentres
Of all you ever knew
In the gradual tornado
By which you cease to know it

In Catalina Park, the pool at Leura,
Where the swan-white flying boat awaited
The next old-fashioned war
I swam on my back and looked up through
Gun blisters as the sunlight burst
On the empty perspex
And now those haloed constellations
Blaze at the basis of my memories
Of Schloss Liliencron,
The sparkling rococo plaster swirls
Of Petrodvoretz,
The shimmer at Sirmione
Where thigh-deep you waded like a nymph
As if Catullus, writing, watched you wade,
– Steve Greenblatt in Cambridge
On the night I first directed

The Pembroke Smoker
Said, "My God, she's beautiful" –
And I think now, as life begins to leave me,
Of the many times I saw that beauty
If only as an echo
Like the pearl farms on the Bay of Toba
Where the sun dissolved the water
Into sheets of silver milk;
A floor of light for the dawn's dancing

I saw that specific glow again
In the glazed floors of the proving grounds
In Nevada, where the mountains cupped
The ground-level theatre
Whose soil and rocks had been
Struck pale green by the nukes:
It was like a sudden close-up
Of those paint-box ponds
That you see from altitude
As the 707 starts

Its crawl across to Sydney
From Perth, as if the landscape
Had plans to be a Nolan.
The desolation of it.
Nullarbor: no trees,
But craters full of colours
That the painters of Florence
Would have given their eye-teeth for.

But where the desert folds
And becomes the opal mineshafts

Of Kalgoorlie, a new sky
Opens beneath the surface.
Invited by the Greek mayor
I rode a bucket down
Through lush flickerings of glory
And once again I was in Luna Park.
Perhaps there's never been a time
When I was somewhere else.
Those Oliver Messel colours
Those pink-tinged midnight blues
Are a cosmic opera house,
A universal panoply of music
Sent down to live in darkness

And always I recall
The collective thrill at Glyndebourne
At the enunciatory chords
When the little mountain opened
And out of that sumptuous interior
The Queen of the Night came racing
To attack, as if her melodies
Were bolts from a death ray,
Her audience dressed to the nines
Reeling in the storm of her cadenzas
The gorgeous bitch.

The brains you take abroad
Acquired their keen propensities
For ravenous exfoliation
A hundred yards from home:
The day I climbed the willow

That overlooked the creek
At the bottom of our street
And caught the Yellow Monday
I was looking at my life
As it pulsed between my fingers:
An ugly little bastard
If you saw only its face
But look into his colours
As beautiful as a sunset
Seen through a burning harvest:
A brooch for the Queen of the Night!

One of my mother's brooches
That she wore when she went dancing
With my father at Cronulla,
In their other life, before the war:
The life they had together
For just that blessed moment,
The life she, and then I, missed so much:
My life, which might have been
A festival of ordinary delights
Has been ruled by my regrets

And how he must have thought
Of that, when, on the docks
Of Kobe, the time came in the day
For the guard called the Mad Doctor
To pick him out and beat him.
A prisoner who got back
Told me of this years later,
And I, who was never well –

Not in my mind, at any rate –
Began my falling further
Into this delirium
Which I trust will end in peace.

Wild cherry logs burning on charcoal,
Jaguar pelts in the Olmec pictograph
Deep in the cold cave that I should have seen
After Carlos Fuentes, in his library,
Sang the praises of Oaxaca.
But my time as a traveller ran out
And I never reached Oaxaca, though perhaps
I have reached it now, Adrastus:
The Olmecs at La Venta
Knowing that they had faded
Made signs to mark their history
As a chronicle, like this,

And during that time Christ was born,
Lived his short life, and died,
Dismantled by the torment.
A chronicle, like this,
Assuming this was what they once had seen
And lived with, like the star-streams overhead
That I can never see from Cambridge
But I saw in the deep desert
Fifty miles outside Las Vegas
Pools of quartz in the fire's light
A darkness only they can own
Their own night
The young Carlos dancing

Who by now has so long left me
As they all have, my fathers and my brothers
They have or else they will –
Felled by the blades that smooth the harvest
Into the ballroom floor
That the angels dance on
And the snowfields of Aspen
In the early morning
After the grumbling diesel ploughs have done
Their night's work
So that the female skiers
In the brilliance of the dawn
Can fishtail through the moguls
With no more than a whisper:

And one of them is you
Who never knew she was
A born *tanguista* –
Condemned to be a scholar
By the duties that burden a bright mind.

If I ever danced again
It would be with you
On the smooth boards of this kitchen.
Shall we try it soon?
Worst that can happen is
I trip over my feet,
You're trapped below my body,
And the *Daily Mail* reporter
Gets here before the police.
It could be a fun scene,

But alas, my legs are heavier
Than a hulking god's at Karnak
And I can barely stumble.

In the ward of ruined men
The thing you will hear most often
Is "I can't do it"
For a thing they'd been doing all their lives
Like putting on a sock.
You hear it *sotto voce*:
It's a private thing
In the hall of mutterings and anger.

Since it was forbidden for a commoner
To die within a mile
Of Versailles, there must have been
One holy mother of a bum's rush
When the sick started walking

And now, at night, on the gravel path
Beside the Seine they pass me
And Marc Bloch is with them
– When I picture him walking
I undo the Gestapo torture,
Because I never did find out
Which bits of him they broke –
And there, handsome as always, is Camus
With his usual platoon
Of pretty women
Perhaps stolen from the King

At Yaralla Hospital
Where my mother used to take me
To visit my cousin Kenny
Who came back from the islands
And did nothing else but waste away

The doctors still called it
Creeping paralysis
Just to make sure
That you knew what you were in for

He would lie there in the iron lung
As if it were his tomb
While the action of the pump
Was taking him away
Simply by the rhythm
With which it kept him there

I could see the fog
On the perfect surfaces
Thickening and thinning
In the *galerie des glaces*
Above his mouth
At the pace of a man walking.
And when, curse me, he came home
To his mother's dining table
I got into deep trouble

When I asked him why
He held his fork
In both hands.

The way he couldn't answer
Made my aunt cry
Until the day he went back in
For keeps, that was the rhythm
A visit to him
A visit from him
And either way
The thing that mattered most
Was his depth of breathing
As we watched him fading

Regard Watteau's morose pierrots –
Or at best equipped with a *fou rire* –
Sibilant in their painted silk:
The embarkation for Cythera
On the double-ended ferry
From Circular Quay
The journey through the mirror
On the old *South Steyne*
To where I am now
In the valley of reflections
That fuse and then dissolve
First the multiplicity –
A storm of definitions –

And then the glow of fire
As the frantic horses burn
In the red light district
Of Hiroshima

Picasso did his best
When he chose his screaming horse

To find the outer limits
Of panic and of pain,
But life would soon outdo him
With chambers full of children
Aware that they were choking
In a fog even their mothers
Would not be able to undo
Qué làstima, ohimè lasso
And far away from them
Two children who escaped
Were me and you

Diderot, loathing Boucher,
Much preferred Chardin
Who liked his luxury austere
And looked like Seamus Heaney
In the Widow Twanky's hat

The personal appearance of the artist
Matters most when it should not
Look at Augustus John
Who was still so handsome
You could not stop doting
When his pictures were going haywire
As his sister Gwen outstripped him.

I can still see Kenny now
Whose fade-out never stopped
Until the day it locked up tight
With nothing left to lose:
His version of paralysis

Was a set of graphs
That made a ghost of him.
As death nears
We all write Kepler's book
The Geometry of Lunar Shadows
The disassembly of the skein of grace
That first was torn to pieces
In the breakers of Avalon
And for fifty years
I have been getting ready
For the echo of the rip-tide
To suck me under

In Proust, when the hero is in Paris
He dreams about Combray
But dreams of Paris when he is in Venice:
A displacement sufficient
For his suave complexity.
In Venice he says he loved Albertine
For the dawn reflected in her face

Malcolm Lowry's lovely title
The Forest Path to the Spring
Has no real story to go with it:
There was no spring, no path, only the forest
Sometimes you just go with the phrase

Just as in this poem
The long path of narration
Is nothing but a forest
Like the trail of images

Collected in the floor
Of Dante's Purgatory
And the trail is made of trails
That alter in the glittering
Squalls of evening
Racing on Sydney Harbour
Where you see the silver lining
Of a single wave
That you will never see again
Until you get to San Francisco.

On this global web of water
On which life, like money spiders,
Blooms in sunlight and withers in the cold
The whisper of the wind
Is the foretaste of the death
Ushering life into existence
Like the ballerinas stepping through the tabs
At the birthday gala
For an ageing monarch
And afterwards, backstage again, I bathed
In the beauty of Merle Park
As if she'd walked out of a waterfall

Merle Park with Nureyev
In the *Nutcracker* pas de deux
That was blocked out by MacMillan
To cut back on the bravura
Except for those two death dives on the trot
When she appears above him
Like a chandelier of cobweb

The impact of a beauty
Echoing through your life

To be seen again in Rio
When the lovely divers
Arriving from Andromeda
Cut their speed to zero

Like a flurry of body blows.
Think back, you feel the thump
And see the circus girl
On her pony in the paddock
But sometimes when the woman could have been
Nureyev's mother
The enchantment was no less
In *Romeo and Juliet*,
Not so much in love with him
As with what her own trajectory
Might well have been if this
Had happened earlier,
Fonteyn came fluttering downstairs
From the tatty balcony
To lie around above his head as if
She were a ripple on the river
Of cruel chronology
And there they were, the sprig for whom
Time hadn't happened yet,
And she who wanted time to stop.

MacMillan staged that pas de deux
For Lynn Seymour

So Fonteyn danced it knowing
That the man who had dreamed up
Those lovely, moth-weight steps
Didn't even want her for the part.
She bit the bullet, kept her dignity,
A quality she had in spades
Where Seymour was all hot sweat and powder.
But MacMillan wasn't in the game
To get his rocks off,
He was in it to make men like me go mad
With the petrol-powered boost
Art gives to sex.

Dealing in such elemental magic
He could be tough, MacMillan:
But then, the whole business of ballet
Is rugged like grid-iron
With bodies broken everywhere.
Flatteringly he wanted
Me to write a spoken script
Something about Nijinsky.
We still would have got nowhere
Even if he'd been well
And he was dying of the plague
But I admired him so much
That I never missed a meeting
And still, today, when it is my turn looming
To plot an exit from the world
Through the glittering corridors
I think of *Mayerling*
On the night when Seymour danced

Her skirt to tatters.
As with Balanchine and Farrell
Beauty was the culprit.
Unable to bear the thought
That she might love her young man
The maestro ruined her career.
He had no excuse whatever:
But I say that just as if
I don't know love,
Its dreadful suddenness.

On the flight from Singapore
Straight down to Perth
When Elle Macpherson
Crossed the aisle to sit beside me
The impact of her beauty
Was exactly like
A mugging from a naiad.
Fame has its privileges
And most of those are drawbacks
But now and then you get to breathe
The aura of the angel –
Occasionally you're dazzled by
The rising of the sun
In the sulphur crest of the white cockatoo

Yet the Chinese women divers never smile
Except when ordered by their commissar
And personally when I dive at night
From the platform or the cliff
And go down ever deeper

Through whatever the dream is,
I go with Tania Cagnotto
Who is not just beautiful
But utterly alive
Like my granddaughter reading
Her *Phoenix* comic –
A smile on fire with energy.

The bamboo bat, no bigger than a bumble bee
Lives in Yunnan
But recalls to me the ladybirds
I once watched in the dunes
When I glanced across the bay
Startled by the tanker's sudden outline
As it passed where the runway would soon
Fill in the blank

Bamboo rats
Tunnel beneath the mulch
Like prisoners on their way
Out of Stalag Luft III
They were gone like Darcy Dugan

Who got himself into the common language
By going absent. Everybody knew
He couldn't be locked up for long.
I, as a kid, would look across to Bunnerong
Where its stacks pumped smoke and power
And I knew that Long Bay gaol was just nearby
And Dugan would soon be gone again.
After his sentencing in Paddo

They locked him into the prison tram
For the trip out to Long Bay
That day he was the only passenger
But when the tram got there and they unlocked it
He wasn't in it.
It was the nth time he escaped
But this time he got into the language:
Gone like Darcy Dugan

The expression "gone like Darcey Bussell"
Has a different resonance
But only slightly:
You get the sense of flying
In both cases

It's a primitive connection
As once the calls of gibbons
Inspired the ancient poets

In Concorde, on its record run
Out to Australia
– The time it had to beat
Was set before the war
So it roughly faced the challenge
Of Usain Bolt
Running about three yards –

When we settled into level flight
Over the Red Sea
I was called to the flight deck,
Settled into the spare seat

Buckled up the way they told me
And looked out across the curve
Of the world
A pharaoh's ring of gold and cobalt
"Yes, it's round all right,"
Said the Captain, something of a wag.
It was the navigator, though,
Who told me by how much
The plane lengthened
When flying at top speed:
It sounded like a mile.
And now I find my life
Is like that, taking far more space
As it speeds towards the end

Like a laden tea-tray clattering downstairs
But doing so entirely on the level
The Concorde bounced along the trail of CAT –
The clear-air turbulence –
Brilliantly it held itself together
While back there in the cabin
They faced their sudden tasks
Of unscrewing the caps
From Lilliputian bottles
And pouring the contents
On crushed ice agitated
By nothing but the outside air.

Dugan and Mears:
When caught after they got out together
Mears was beaten

Until he couldn't walk
And now I have his legs

Nietzsche called Kant
A catastrophic spider.
There was a time after the war
When the chimneys of Auschwitz
Survived their buildings
Like columns at Karnak
Proving that every human thing
Including hell
Begins with a prospect of the Nile
Where the crocodiles are sacred
For being absolutely
The last thing you, when weary,
Would want to meet.

Abu Simbel
Built during amateur night
At the Folies on the Rocks
Is bad at proportion
The knees of the giants
Look bigger than their faces
Toes the size of camper vans

There have to be
Whole eras of false emphasis
Before you reach the scribe
In the Cairo museum
Who strikes us as like us

And he could be me, that scribe:
Bits missing from his skull
Where once my cancers were
That were hammered in like nails
By the sun of the Pacific,
The sky mallet.
In his billboard fresco
We see Rameses II
Mowing down like wheat
His infinite supply
Of victims so outclassed

We might think them willing
But the chances are he got
His throat slit by the women
Of his own harem
At which point, one recalls
That the faience *shabtis* weigh like
Vibrators with no batteries:
Sex, they were nuts about it
Life was the death of them
And is for us.

The purple flowers of Petropolis
Bloom in the *floresta*
Where Stefan Zweig destroyed himself
Having been for too long menaced
By everything, including safety
You could threaten the poor bastard
Even with peace, with time to write,
With blooms like sapphire pinwheels

By Fabergé
Dotting the jungle as if put in place
Specifically to touch his heart

The only time, Spinoza, that your share
Of *natura naturans* comes to balance
Is now. The Sphinx is a test that we must fail
Because she sets no riddle,
Silver gold greens blues
Heads of temple scribes

When you showed me the *Breviario Grimani*
And I wanted to be born again
As Antonello da Messina
The steps to the Marciana
Are still my memory
Of the way to Wonderland
Coffin fragments clogged like coffee grounds
Workshops at the temple of the god Amun
At Karnak Luxor,
As now I scan the chapels leading
Off the longest corridor
Of Addenbrooke's
Between the Outpatients vestibule
And the portico
Of the main hospital
Which, putting out more annexes,
Will one day stretch all the way
To Scotland. Once I could walk it,
Now I must be pushed
And just to turn and look

Is an exhausting effort
But gradually, as the wings and walks advance
They call the decorators in
And almost any previous dull stretch
Becomes a rich collection
Of pictures that redeem
The illusion of randomness
One piece at a time

It's not the National Gallery
Where you see, in the far distance,
That Gainsborough married couple
Out walking on the land
Which all belongs to them.
This land belongs to us,
In its very randomness
And started long ago
Its journey here
Since only to your weary eyes
Could it make sense:

Jigsaw patterns of woodwork
Coffin fragments beneath varnished paintwork
Recycled valuable wood pieces
Acacia and sycamore-fig,
Cedar and Christ's-thorn *sedr* frame
Gold-yellow background
As if from the bath robe
Of a towering Klimt prince
Getting his rocks off in between
The breasts of a great lady,

Surface shine of pistachio tree resin
Brushes, reed pens, pigments
Heated scrap copper, the quartz saw
The maple glade, salts
Blue and green, glassy
Egyptian blue (for the Italians
Precious as indigo)
Blue the colour of a god's hair on his coffin
And mummy masks
Preparing surfaces one colour at a time

Blue goes on last
Before the varnishing:
White and blue that mimic
Brushed silver and bar gold
A divine realm glimpsed
Through joinery and chemistry
And all is rocking slightly
As the wheelchair's wheels
Cope with the turns
The shivers of the world
Where now you have no power
But still must see,
Remembering what love was still
As you cease to be.

In *Les Enfants du Paradis*
The fight between Arletty and María
Casarès for Baptiste's twee adoration
(I'm a Lemaître man, but you could tell)
Is unfairly tilted

In Arletty's favour
"If all the people who lived together
Were in love, the Earth would shine
Like the sun." That girl could talk
Like Jacques Prévert and her shoulders
Were spring snow; no wonder she was catnip
For the nicer type of Nazi.

When the war was over
And the touring entertainers
Who had been sent from France
Came back from Germany
Nobody except Chevalier
Pretended he'd been gathering
Intelligence; he had, of course,
Been losing it, the poor dumb bastard,
With his would-be charming pout,
Although *Love Me Tonight*
His pre-war musical in Hollywood
Directed by Mamoulian
Was the genuine beginning
Of our modern miracle,
The musical whose camera
Flew like a bird. (It didn't last forever:
It's just too hard to do.
Notice how in *Moulin Rouge*
The fluidity comes mainly
From the edits.) But still Tati had been
A better bet, and still today
I dote on M. Hulot.
When things go darker still among the darkness

I dream that it is I, in his canoe,
Who is swallowed by a canvas shark
And when he serves at tennis
It reminds me that sometimes the mad pose
Is all that there is left
And needs your full assurance,
To underpin the chaos
This poem had its impulse
In the way Hulot looks frantic
When the fireworks erupt
The delicious grace of his confusion
As he runs twelve ways at once.
Barrault, though a slick mover, was too swish
To ever be my hero:
Far too flimsy, too much poise,
Too much pose. A man should occupy
The air around him at his ease.
I always loved how Henry Fonda stood
And the first Steve McQueen.

Today, in *Marseille*, Depardieu snorts coke
The camera locked behind his hulking head
Sees nothing but a mountain sniffing up
The corpse of a white mouse
And for a moment this is Karnak
The giant figures wasted by the winds

Depardieu must have been sculpted
By an air-drill and two dredgers
From an outcrop of hot rock

Climbing on Uluru
If you fumble on the rope
And fall it really isn't
All that steep
Just a flailing scramble
All the way to safety
Like my staircase down to breakfast
Where my elder daughter
Eventually arrives
To make the toast

And there, deep in the desert,
Where Australia elevates
Its only true cathedral,
I saw that the hotel terrace
Was full of centipedes
Who sounded like a fry-up on fast forward
The clearest indication
That death would mean erosion

Drewett as Adrastus, on the Mara:
Me and my dear producer taking five
On the empty river bank,
After I almost got killed
By the hulking crocodile,
When we sat in those cane chairs
To watch flamingos landing
And taking off
The place was like Heathrow
With better weather
An invisible control tower

And no duty-free:
Drewett, the world's expert
On what could be accumulated
In the airport sales halls,
Realised, getting ready to go home,
That what we saw would be the only treasure:
You had to take your loot in visions,
And best of them was birds like jiffy bags
On stilts that spilled pink powder –
A walking cloud of them, pick up your feet.

There must be somewhere in the mind
A mechanism fine-tuned to remember
Numerousness
Somewhere between a concept and a threat
When I was young and travelling with my mother
In a train to Armidale through textbook
Rolling hills
One of the rolling hills rolled extra
And headed for the horizon:
It was a sea of kangaroos.

Today I get exactly the same kick
From low-level aerial footage
Of a zillion wildebeest
Spooked by a pride
Of lions and running to escape the commentary
Of David Attenborough
Who airily concludes
There are far too many humans

But in the natural world
There is a benevolence to many-ness.

It would help to see all the snow-leopards left
Crowd a single ridge like an audience
For an early evening charity event
At the Met and suddenly
My mind is full of all the mass assemblies
Of living creatures that I have regarded
As luxuries even when on their own:
Mass rallies of meerkats, torrents of field mice,
Those penguins of the Antarctic islands
That pour themselves into the booming ocean
Like blubbering rubble
Mere cocktail snacks for here-comes-trouble orcas
Cetaceans with such shitty personalities
They punish baby seals for being cute
And enjoy the role of torturer
With the typical dumb glee
Of those whose power
Is their solitary attainment,
Sheer muscle their dimension
The only appropriate reaction
Is by Spencer Tracy
In *Judgment at Nuremberg*—
An infinite regret.

But in the greatest on-screen dialogue
Ever to feature Dietrich
She did not appear at all
Accepting that her looks were gone for good

Maximilian Schell
Just interviewed her voice.
It was a funeral in Berlin

Heading for England through the Sunda Strait
I thought, while the porpoises were hurdling
The swell to the forefront of the ship,
"There, then, we won't be running out
Of porpoises."
I think I wrote a poem about that lot
But I'm starting to forget.
Of course I am
Every lyrical memory
I ever had is by now fleeing
Towards where the sky turns into jewellery
And anyway when I think
Of that district now
I think of Perth.

The year that I was born
The cruiser *Amphion* transferred
To the RAN and got her new name *Perth*
She went to the World's Fair in New York
There's a photo of her in the Panama Canal
On March 31, 1940 she was tied up
At Garden Island and my mother might
Have seen her
On the night of March 28–29
She was at Matapan
She sank in the Sunda Strait
And lent her fame

To the city she was named for
The city famous for being somewhere
Where nothing had ever happened.
The poet Harry Hooton
– I saw him once, at the Royal George Hotel –
Wrote an immortal mini-epic poem.
I give you the whole thing:
"In the midst of life
We are in Perth."

And the house came down
As it did at Kakadu
Where I watched a fat man in a flat bush hat
Haul out a barramundi
That was bigger than his little boat
And him put together,
While nearby our helicopter
Went skirting the escarpment
Like a scolding skua screaming
The place down when a wave
Stone-walls, and drops of foam
Whistle like bullets

After our quiz-kid class transferred to Hurstville
And School Swimming switched to Ramsgate Baths
Our teacher Mr Leonard, giving us
Something to aim at, threw back somersaults
From the low board. Forever in full thrall
To his fine example, I have rarely mentioned it
Before today. In the war he navigated
Lancasters all the way to Germany

And back. A terrific teacher,
So why, till now, have I always left him out,
Except for the occasional fleeting name-check?
The answer is too easy and still too daunting.
The ideal father figure, he raised the question,
Simply by being there, of what life would have been
Like if my father had come home.
The answer is still spinning, like a man
In space. When he went into the water
His thumbs were lightly placed beside the seams
Of his swimming trunks as if it were no effort,
Just a routine acknowledgment of neatness,
As an ideal, the way I still think now
That rhymes should be.

And why is he appearing only now, long later?
The secret of the effort I have put
Into forgetting him for these three quarters
Of a century has to be he was so clearly
The answer to my wish.
È una festa, la mia vita,
Says Guido to Luisa
In *Otto e mezzo*:
Arrogant even in apology
As befits his character.

The equinox is near, and in the windows
Of the infusion clinic shines a soft spring light
With a twinge of the cannula
In my wrist I stir from sleep
Young Shaista has arrived

As radiant as always, though her lupus
Is seldom long fought off.
It is the wolf that runs at random.
And eats the contents of the mini-market
Somewhere along the road to Nome, Alaska
Or in the shopping mall at Oodnadatta.
One day, to disabuse me
Of my sentimental faith
That all would be well for her
– She being beautiful, I thought
Damage would be undone
By one of those divine rules
That I know do not exist –
She held back an eyelid so that I could see
The bleb that held one of her eyes in place:
A miracle of metal
That had travelled here to help her
Across the concentrated universe
Of time that we call science.
And there, in a silver gleam,
Is God,
Or, put it another way, there is
No more of God than this.
Believe me, Adrastus,
That if there were a heaven
We would see it in her smile.

Of all the sacred books, it must be Dante
That is the most so; but if I only chose
A single sacred book, that single object
Would be the *Breviario Grimani*.

You brought me to it in that year in Venice
Before we were yet married
When there was so much light on the lagoon
It was like looking at the sun.
You had prepared me well for the *Breviario*,
Telling me little, letting the impact come
As an undiluted shock.
With your scholarly credentials
You were allowed upstairs
At the Marciana, and could bring
A guest. I was the guest, as I am in this poem,
Which is your gift to me.

Up the marble steps
I followed you, while noting
As I always noted when
You walked in summer, that you were
A very fine example
Of a young Australian woman
Dressed for the light's heat
As if the sun pumped luminance
Even in the cool room of the stairwell
Sangallo gave the library, as its key motif,
The monumental splendour of the ascent
To knowledge: this way to the lovely books.
And with your scholar's entrée we would see
The book of books. It was brought out to us
And placed with all due care as if its beauty
Were sensitive to air and any sky
That still stuck to our fingertips:
The *Breviario Grimani*

Page after page
Of miniatures and even the print columns
Proportioned and illuminated
Like trays of jewels

In Grigson's fine account
Sir Humphry Davy watches
"The glittering particles of potassium
Breaking through the potash crust"

As Whitman, at the very end
Of *Leaves of Grass*,
Talks, with his voice fading
At long last,
"Undismayed among the rapids"
Of "the divine ship, the world",
Long ago in my life now, by now back there
Near the beginning,
In the Sunda Strait, the porpoises
Crest-hurdling towards the setting sun
Gave those of us transfixed at the ship's rail
Their most convincing demonstration
That they'll be with us on the day
We leave the dying Earth.

In just that way I plunged, with your sweet guidance,
Into the beauty of that book
As the miniatures revealed one at a time
Their meticulous opulence
And still, today, there has been nothing else
To move me like the butterfly

Splendour of Antonello,
Except, of course, in nature
And art is nature too
And will be even when
Machines begin to do it
Without needing to be told

For machines impose their order
And even a library is a soft machine
As once the library was in Alexandria
Stacking its books in colonnades
And passageways

In Sydney now, on long shelves underground
I melt into the catalogue
In just the way that library in Bohemia
Where I read Metternich
Will double as a dust-bath
When the time comes for books to fall apart

At Boa Vista in Cape Verde:
Sea turtles nest ashore
The hump-backed whales cruise by
Like various components
Of the Flying Scotsman

Brown tufted capuchins emerge
Each of them an adept
Of the husked nut
The husk dried in the sunlight for a week
Hammering the husk takes eight long years to learn
And then you get a smile of pride

Like mine on the day I first read Pushkin
In the original and madly pretty language
But it wasn't *Eugene Onegin*:
It was *The Three Bears*.

The stalk-eyed fly pumps up his eyes
To get girls, widest eye-span gets the girl
The winner gets them all
When the male rhino gets stuck in mud
All of his females leave, for they
Are good-time floozies.
The chin-strap penguin chick is caught and crushed
By the hefty skua

A chameleon in the desert
Goes darker on one side
The lost explorer
Who thought the little beast might be a compass
For walking north to Cairo
Has walked south to Khartoum.
What a turn-around.

Remembering how Arletty sparkled
In her starlit bolero
As Carné's camera framed her
Puts you with Delphine Seyrig
On the balcony in Marienbad
The black and white photography spoke colours
The colours of the night
In those days I could play the match game
And played it cool, like Sacha Pitoëff

Somehow I never realised
Detachment from the world
Was the wrong idea for me
I was an involved one
I wanted everything
And I will leave the world
In a cloud of a million tendrils
That once joined me to everything
Even the drifting pollen

Sky burial at Kailash
The nuns who feed the pheasants
Help prepare the soil
That will consume the dead.
The escape from this ritual is enlightenment
Black-necked cranes stand no more than an inch
Deep in the stygian water
And the shine on the water is a sky painting
While children propel the prayer-wheels
By playing on them. At that rate, Luna Park
Must have been a sacred engine
For half the universe.
The sickness that I felt
When running through the barrel
Whose halves went different ways
(If you didn't skip you fell)
Was a worm-hole to Andromeda
But when I told my mother
That I wished my father could see me
As I proudly ran the course
She was hurt so terribly

That I always kept the secret
Though I didn't even know
In those days
That all M31 –
A starry wheel at least as big as us –
Was on its way here anyway
She only had to wait
For umpteen million years
And one day they'd be in amongst each other
The two events, twin multiplicities,
The blending of always and forever

Like the shoals of fragile
British and German fighters
Interpenetrating over Abbeville
In the days when a plane weighed not much more
Than the man who flew it
A few mechanics could pick up a *Dreidecker*
And put it over there.
The sky awaits, Red Baron.

And always, like the voice of Lars von Trier
On the soundtrack of *Europa*,
I go back to Luna Park
For more of my last visit
That has led to here.

Where was I? In the River Caves
On the street of castles
Where they have their frontages
On a Grand Canal
Or it could be the Fontanka.

It all blends here
Because it all ends here.

When my father's body
Sits up in the fire
And forms an echo of the monk
Who burned in Vietnam
As if to say, "This changes
Everything. From this
You will not come back."

Vyacheslav Tikhonov in the Bondarchuk
Movie of *War and Peace*
Ringing the bell of what one wants to look like
When clapping eyes for the first time
On Natasha Rostova
As any man must do
To leave the world:
That final revelation
Of absolute young beauty
Is your ticket out

The light comes edging through the purple clouds
Like burnished silver foliage on Roman capitals
And we flinch below the pent-up scoops of water:
Rain getting set to happen

As Claudius brought those cool streams into Rome
On aqueducts and made a water city
Almost as Venice later was
There where Bartolomeo
Colleoni rides his mighty war-horse

On a plinth above the water
As if the floods of Florence
Had reached him, or as if
The floods of Una Voce
Had reached out from the Hawkesbury
And had joined it to the Arno

Ama No Gawa
The River in the Sky
The way the Japanese
Say Milky Way
Is just another flood
The way that *Perché No?*
Was annexed to paradise
And *La Lucciola Estiva*
(The Summer Firefly)
Was waiting in the riverbed
To show us once again
Quel treno per Yuma
And the way Glenn Ford
Fell for Felicia Farr

I realise you have been in this poem
And observing it as well,
But that anomaly is true to life

Within the decorated borders
Of the magic book
The enchanted houses and the great
Ladies and their daughters

Flocks a murmuration of starlings
The congregations at the poles
Of the bar magnet
The corroborees of iron filings
Echo within perceptions
Like the Almagest of Ptolemy

As Kafka's *Nachlass* scintillates before us
Lit by the fire that Max Brod did not light
Walled by the books that were not burned

In a bid for oblivion that was as pointless
As the edict of Tiberius
Against promiscuous kissing

On *Gardener's World*
The lady presenter
Strafed by the poetry from all directions
– She must feel that she is being
Shot to pieces
By Technicolor tracer –

Hails primroses, the epitome of spring,
The stars of April

The BBC sound engineer
Toting his blimped-up microphone
As he walks in rubber boots
Through the flat-lands of the Wash –
The mud-lands, the lands of the sodden grass,
The cushy pampas –

Says he sometimes thinks that the dead go
Into the wind.
Geese put their flaps down
And wobble down to land,
Pipits head for where the sea starts
He hears it all and stores it
For his wild-track, the murmur without people,
He's got it there on tape
The set of interweaving murmurations
My mind is now becoming
That once was clear for being simple

In the far Pacific
On three new tropical islands
The mouse lemurs are still evolving
They will probably end up with keyboards
For teeth, and whiplash aerials
For whiskers.

In Hawaii, with all its islands younger
Than any continent,
The nectar-feeding honeycreepers
Are not great flyers
Too far adapted from the finch
They can get from flower to flower
And maybe from one island to the next:
But let's not ask them for the moon

And suddenly it's now
And now will soon be gone
And everything depends

On Jennifer Doudna's father
Leaving a copy of *The Double Helix*
On his clever daughter's bed.
This, also, happened in Hawaii,
So calculate the chances.
We are dying, Egypt, dying –
But from bewilderment

A hammerhead, the male drosophila
Like all the species of his genus
Has descended from a single female five
Millennia ago, so call her Madam.
The inchworm caterpillars, when deprived
Of food, will eat each other
Because they can't revert.
They're saddled with the harsh word "obligate"
Because forbidden to go back and start
Again, poor mites. The spider that rejoices
In the name of Orsonwelles, no hyphen:
The camera takes one look at him and there
We are, in the Prater of Vienna,
Betting his web is like the Ferris wheel
And that he hears
The chimes at midnight

The lava lake which is impossibly
Called Puʻu ʻŌʻō
Started a hundred kilometres down
And as the earth turns, craters form a string
Of cameos in bubbling liquid rock
While spaced out in the fields of cooling magma

Are the clumps of spines called silversword
Which turns out when it flourishes and dies
To be a bone-dry daisy
And not the battle-spear you might imagine,
Though it looks fit to be carried to the war
By Crazy Horse

As the tree ferns of Hawaii reach their height
In fields of naked lava
The nene geese fly above them but between
The islands only,
When once they roamed the southern world.
The special task that finances your life
You pay for when it pins you to the spot,
So travel when you can.
A lizard like a miniature triceratops
With nothing to prey on it
Eats everything it finds
The honeycreeper is found anywhere
Mosquitoes aren't

I like to hear the scientists
Who say the first Mars ship might have to land
Sideways. Such a perfect *Goon Show* concept,
With Space Vice-Admiral Eccles in command!
I don't expect the ship to leave
Before I'm gone. Even if they start now
It will take so long to build.
But already there is talk
Of Mars-station personnel who volunteer
Not to come home. I was expecting that,

Though personally I have enjoyed the world
So much I'd sign on for another lifetime,
As long as my granddaughter flies the ship

As now she flies my wheelchair
Glittering in its crimson
Along my corridor
And onward into orbit
What happens next
Will surely validate
What Matthew Arnold called
The barren optimistic sophistries

"How short life must be," said frightened Kafka
About a woman's body
"If something so fragile can last a lifetime."
There are moments in *Shooter* when the waistline
Of Kate Mara framed closely from the back
Reminds me precisely of the bow
That I made from a willow wand in 1950.
It wasn't fragile but the arrows were.
They were made from reeds.
Kogarah, my stamping ground,
Means "Place of Reeds",
And the mini-swamp between the park
And Ramsgate Baths
Was my first idea of jungle.

A daunting prospect even when looked back on,
When you consider that all the jungles full
Of creatures killing each other

Must be releasing as much energy
As the Battle of Kursk –
Though I suppose you should count the oceans in
With every great white rating as a Tiger tank.

"Be strong, my wife," says the TV Spartacus
As they gaze out from the mountains
At the photogenic sunset
(Merely remember Daniel Day-Lewis
And Madeleine Stowe in the lyrical finale
Of *Last of the Mohicans*
And wrap them in a Roman-era
Car-coat each). Their faces face the flame
While Spartacus adds weirdly
"Keep me close to your thighs"
In a battle scene there is an eloquent
Explanatory subtitle: "Urgh."
So speaks a hero in extremis.
I should not mock, because the dialogue
Of unabashed exposition
Is among my fall-back art-forms:
Something I could write were incapacity
To take the last reserves of my hard-earned.
"Does your father know you're in Thrace?"
I hear these things with ears attuned by now
To the hum of a plump dove
Fluffily eyeing up his secretary
On my back fence.
She must think "What a ham"
But plays it cool.

At breakfast on my terrace in late spring
My elder daughter is the first to notice
The arrival of our favourite robin red-breast,
Fat-boy Freddie. Newly stocked
With seeds, the bird feeder also has
Meal worms, who possibly made an error
By allowing that tag to be hung on them.
Anyway that's my daughter's theory.
Straining to get its box-car body airborne
The robin leaves, as if to join its regiment
Of guards. This starling, on the other hand,
Is definitely a private soldier.
A blackbird stalks on stage as if arriving from
That movie that I once saw as a kid,
In which there were no humans.
Not liking very much the whole idea
Of animals as actors, I sat it out
With small enthusiasm. In my view
Anthropomorphism belongs to people
And the snow leopard death-diving down the cliff
Can only remind you of von Richthofen
Attacking from the clouds above Arras
If you remember it does not speak German.

I think, then, of the thinker Michael Tanner
And the range of philosophical credentials
He brings to his exultant imitation
Of Schwarzkopf in her masterclasses pursing
Her lips to screw her demo of the umlaut
To the sticking point of sheer absurdity,
And then, my train of thought a runaway,

Of her and Christa Ludwig and Teresa
Stich-Randall in the surging, soaring trio
From the last act of *Rosenkavalier*
As I played the disc until
The vinyl started turning white
Like coal eaten by acidic snow

My friend Locantro, working at EMI,
Told me how the greatest Salome
Of all time, Ljuba Welitsch,
Answered the awkward question
Of whatever had happened to her voice:
"Too much cock."

Time comes for the great soprano
As it comes, too, for the crepe-soled rock'n'roll star
With the ice-cream cow-lick,
And I who was born to love them all
Must now resign myself to every variation
Of the long goodbye.

At Sydney Stadium for Bill Haley and the Comets
I particularly relished, among the glazed refinements
Acquired by a century of touring,
How the double bass player
Turned his giant instrument on its edge
Before he climbed aboard and launched
Into his solo
While Haley, rocking along beneath his wig,
Smiled as if he had never seen before
Anything so witty in his life:

Not high art perhaps, that kind of thing:
But it does establish
The perennial place in history
Of steak-raw energy:
The spring of joy
Which even Michelangelo must have felt
When he got the notion
Of making his prisoner float from the tomb.

Out on my Malvern Star
To explore the hangars at Mascot –
The airport still officially
Called Kingsford Smith
In those days, and only later Sydney –
I found in one of the big dark sheds –
Not working hangars any more,
Just hold-all areas for junk –
The *Southern Cross*, the Fokker Trimotor
That Smithy flew on his adventures.
What I remember most today
Is how the deep blue paint-job
Was almost like the dark around it.
Between its life and death there was a blending
As, in that poem by poor Francis Webb,
Sunset hails a rising.

Somewhere between Allahabad
And Singapore
Over the Andaman Sea
Smithy winked out for good.
For everyone from my part of the world
He remains the complete air hero,

Though personally I favour
Jean Batten, New Zealand's darling daughter,

Whose portraits, doe-skin helmets or whole aircraft
Are in all the Kiwi airports.
From any angle and in any context
She was absolutely lovely,
Which should not be a factor
But presumably, even among seagulls, is.

Ida Nossuk had the nuclear fusion insight
Before any of the men
And Muriel Whedale Onslow
Intuited the orderly progression
In the colours of the flowers.
Lise Meitner observed the stately process
By which her Nobel prize went to Otto Hahn.
In my own mind, each and every atom
Belongs to Greer Garson
In her role as Queen Marie Curie.
Rosie Franklin would have had a perfect right
To come back from the dead and light a fire
Under Crick and Watson in either order.
It's a women's world
I think, no doubt because
When I was young the women did
All the deciding, as if the men
Would be away forever.
And then it turned out that one was
And my universe fell in
And started its long journey to Andromeda.

The eloquent magnificence
In Rustodiev's neo-baroque full-length
Portrait of Chaliapin
Is like the singer's voice made visible
And sometimes you can see the same hauteur
Still there when people leave,
As you still see Garbo's omnicompetence
Her divine housewifely sense of order
In pictures of the apartment that she bought
In 1950, taking the whole fifth floor
Of the Campanile co-op. The master bedroom
Of a woman without a master
Had Fortuny silken linings
Steadily impregnated with her solitude
Until she died at eighty-four. And still she is Ninotchka
When you look at the things she chose
To populate the space
With no one except herself,

And her view of the East River
Is Ninotchka too. Ken Tynan loved that speech:
Bomps may fall . . . We have had our moment.
So always when I think of her I think
Of Tynan, on his lilo in the sunlight
Of the canyon in LA, reading aloud
From Hemingway, that bit about the Gulf Stream
Absorbing all the offal and the garbage
Yet after a certain time of contemplation
Still running pure. But Ken was talking about
His dying dreams, of course: he knew his lungs
Were choked and soon would kill him.

He had his oxygen beside him and I wondered
How I would cope if my breath would not come.
Today I almost know
But not quite yet

There is so much to enjoy.
Alberto Manguel tells us
That when, in the tenth century,
The Grand Vizier of Persia
Travelled with all his books
(He had 117 thousand of them)
They were carried by a caravan
Of 400 camels trained to walk
In alphabetical order.
This news makes me want to write
A book called *Aardvark Archives of Australia*.
Thus to satisfy a profound conviction
Admittedly, let's face it, psychopathic,
That I basically belong on the first camel.

Like the Americans in Vietnam
The French lost in Algeria
Because they had a home to go to

As was said by that philosopher Massu
The realities of war were
Peu connue aux échelons supérieurs
And the French might have kept Algeria
For ever
If, once a fortnight

Massu and the paratroopers
Had arrived to parade down the main drag
As in *The Battle of Algiers*
Where Pontecorvo caught exactly
The doomed triumphalism
That looks so good in camouflage

War is when
The foot-flagging frog
Meets the Aussie spider with the headlights

Ostriches when running
Have the loping Olympic look
Of Emil Zátopek
They need only the shoes

Hermit crabs that constantly trade up
For a bigger shelter
Should see the road ahead as nothing but
A chain of opportunities
More likely though, they think each change
Of domicile
As the one, the only, life-defining struggle
Just don't let them tell you about it

Star clusters spill, in visual form
The exquisite Mark Knopfler melodies
Of the Dire Straits first albums
The guitar lick weary with its beauty

There is a small fat male fish
That turns himself into a rose window
At least six feet across
Purely to impress the female
Who signals, "What you did then:
Do you think you could do
That thing again?"
But he's exhausted

A small shark like the epaulette
Of a Ruritanian band leader
Slips through the cracks
Of a reef's drying offshoot

Behold the pygmy marmoset
OK, where is it?

Filmed from high up
H-bombs being tested were the jellyfish
That used to gather in Sans Souci baths
In a clear attempt to stop me jumping
From the ten-foot tower.
I would watch them pullulating in the water
Like a garden of evil
Until I picked a spot between them
That would let me in
And down I came, exactly like a vandal,
To smash a window that did not exist.

Yves Klein dying at thirty-four
Left a mark that was all his

Or almost so
A splash of ultramarine
Exactly the same for vividness
As fills the flutes in the gold mask
Of Tutankhamun.
While the kid was splashing on his gouts
Of that sumptuously enchanting colour
Even New York was heading back to Egypt
Klein was so frail that he was never
Not almost dead
But when you see that burst of blue
Like a barrel-bomb of Hokusai's
Aizuri ichimai
It's like a truck
Running wild downtown
Or a dolphin in your bathtub.
The letters of Peierls' wife to Klaus Fuchs
Were a sea of ink:
She never guessed that he was lying.
My wife is like that.
Honest, she thinks the world is honest too

When Guillaume de Machaut
Puts his *douce dame jolie*
Into that pretty suite of sound
We hear how love
Can build a garden
Out of pure forms
And gash your heart
With the edge of a rose petal

But for any artist of any kind
Nothing is harder
Than to catch the power
Of tenderness:
In the documentary sequence
That sets up James Cameron's *Titanic*
A bunch of actors registering awe
At the worst drawing of a woman
In the history of the world
Still pay it silent tribute,
And you never know, they might be right
If all the beauty of the earth begins
As a charcoal study by Leonardo DiCaprio
Before time happens to it
And it turns into Kate Winslet

Imagine the first sketches
For Helen of Troy
Not even close
But in merely a couple of thousand years
We say it could be her
The very one
Who, after Paris was slain,
Married Deiphobus,
But who remembers that?
Easier to remember
The best screen Helen
Rossana Podestà
Who once was just a kid
Parked at a table on the Via Veneto
Pointing her miraculous bazookas

At the paparazzi
But up there in a hundred or so square metres
Of dripping Warnercolour
She launched a thousand ships.

I should say at this point, though,
That every cameo and coin profile
Of Cleopatra looks like perfect hell.
She's Mike Mazurki's brother.
For purposes of emphasis
I could have said she must have looked
Like Leelee Sobieski at the very least,
Or else the experienced Antony
Would have sailed on the first tide
For Rome and triumph:
But this is, at the last, an honest poem.

Though I say this as a master sergeant
In the front rank of the Philistines,
What hope did the atonal
Composers think they had?
I haven't yet run out
Even of Bach cantatas
And there's only a few hours left to me.

Though I should, and I admit this,
Do something about Messiaen
And I never even really knuckled under
To Bruckner, let alone Varese.
I could go on, except I can't:

Too little oomph left even to put names
To the gaps of knowledge that I know are there
Forming a second silence like dark stars.

My world is closing in on me, and soon
The time must come when most of the exploring
Will be done by you, if it is not confined
To these books in this room and the neat garden
Outside those doors. Already it was you
That went down to Bilbao and walked inside
The hall where Richard Serra built his maze
From the peelings of a rusty giant apple –
Or let them be the florets of a sunflower –
So that they add up to a space-filled solid
Like the shaped hull of a nautilus crushed under
The good heel of Achilles. Though no pictures
Are allowed to visitors, I still see you
Drifting alertly through the sea of pieces,
Taking it in, as if the future's ruins
Were there for you to study. These mis-shapes
The artist made by chance, if not from love,
Accumulate to raise the niggling question
Of what the abstract is, and when its time
Has come. It comes when art disintegrates,
You might conclude: explosive force
Propels the drift of shapes through the deep sea.
Serra does not love Gehry, that's for sure:
He talks about the architect as if
To demonstrate that Michelangelo
Was right to stint his praise for Raphael.
But you are well used to the awkward fact

Not even the Renaissance had the room
To hold all those hulking personalities
Without their shells colliding. Seen from now
It all clicks like a wave, but at the time
They fought for space as we do. Hence my trust
That you are the ideal appreciator
Of what will happen, what is happening, next:
Precisely since it cannot be predicted.
So go again, then, there to walk among
The walls of Babylon and Berlin's ruins
All in the one great room, which, on the outskirts
Of oblivion, asserts our sense of form
As a broken cry of triumph.

When finally the old painters all go down
– Titian, Rembrandt, Turner, Hokusai –
Under the wave off Kanagawa,
Saying they want just five more years, just five
To become an artist –
Like needing just a couple
Of colossal amber buttons
Sewn on a clockwork mouse
To become the littlest lemur –
It's maybe time to quit.

In Paris, Terry Southern and Miles Davis –
The triumvirate completed by Charlie Mingus –
All went to see *L'Avventura*,
The coolest thing on screen in 1960.
In the longest of the long, long stretches when
The hero fails to find his missing girlfriend,

I can hear Miles, with the mutely strangled style
That turned his every sketch of Spain
Into the small cry of a dying gerbil,
I can hear Miles, sitting in the dark,
Going "peep peep, peep peep peep, peep peep"
And Mingus going "doom, ba-doom ba-doom"
While Southern, coming round from a deep sleep,
Says, "What the holy fuck is happening here?"
The actor was Gabriele Ferzetti
(Girl-sounding name, great-looking guy)
And the actress who went missing, Lea Massari,
Never complained she was left out of view
While Vitti became every grown man's dream
Of the well-bred, elegant Italian female
With the slightly open mouth.
Today she is no longer on my mind
And her lover Antonioni isn't either,
Nor Miles – maybe a little bit – nor Mingus.
But Southern's cool book *Red-Dirt Marijuana*
Is still one of my everlasting touchstones
For how non-fiction pieces ought to sound:
Allusive, rhythmic, fact-filled and poetic
Like the hip talk of a bunch of Yanks in Paris,
Blasé but hungry for sophistication,
The way that even Bleecker St will make you
Long for that café near the Sorbonne

Yet little of the best wit comes from literature.
The concert hall is far the better bet.
Quite apart from all those cracks by Beecham,
Richard Strauss advised conductors

Never to look at the trombones.
"It only encourages them."

The scholarship will always underestimate
The way the classical goes back to pop.
It is an eternal return. The symphonies
Of that glorious, rich century before last,
Would always have a song-show in them somewhere
Stolen from the echoes of street vendors.
The tragedy that Schoenberg incarnates
In my view, was his willed determination
To forget all that. So little to draw you in:
A spine forest without a single peacock.

And yet remember this: when he and Gershwin
Lived near each other in Beverly Hills,
Not only the ageing exile but the blessed
New boy was keen for a game of tennis
Perhaps they heard a symphony for strings
That they could share,
Though no one could have guessed
That fate would come first for the prodigy
And kill him. I do not want to be gone.
For once I feel it, feeling young again.

The Everly Brothers before they both left school
In Shenandoah, Iowa
Could sing the way two seagulls
Would sing if they could charm the waves
As they flew through the loping troughs and crests

In Havana that morning
I sat in a corner of the Floridita
Getting in the mood
To penetrate the heart of Papa-land
And then I went by cab to the Finca Vigía.
First thing I saw
Was the *Pilar* up on blocks
And then I climbed the back steps of the house.
Nobody was allowed in,
But you could stand in the verandah
Look through the glass into the living room
And there they were: the books
Still neatly ranked
As if he might come back some night
And check up on a reference to Turgenev.
I scanned the shelves for spines
Of novels by Ronald Firbank
But couldn't find them. I knew, though,
That they had to be there somewhere.
One of the things that made him great
Was his taste for stylists
Whose style was not like his.

I bathed in the radiated neatness
Of thousands of titles
But the sight that moved me most
Was a pair of moccasins
Out there on the carpet like a couple of canoes
Set to take someone bigger than the Yeti
Into the mist that cloaks the waterfall
Of unremitting, ever-extending time,

Which, captured in its density and essence
Will outrun even death.

Energy: some people have just got it,
Though by now it feels like they have taken mine.
In Chicago, bearding Solti in his den
At the opera house, I found him bearding me.
I told him truly that back there in England
My wife was wearing out *Eugene Onegin*,
But he turned the tables and poured guttural praise
On my first book of memoirs. In despair
At shooting stuff we couldn't use, I slunk away
To the empty auditorium and took a seat
As he had instructed me. The orchestra
Came streaming in and took their many places
On stage. They finished tuning up
And on he walked.

He looked around and winked. We caught the wink
On film, and what the orchestra did next
We caught on sound. You guessed: it was the first
Few mighty bars of *Thus Spake Zarathustra*.
I was set to hear it all but the maestro heard
A dud note, called a halt and gently bollocked
The third viola from the left.

He was a lovely man though. Last time I saw him
Was at Buck House for a Royal birthday.
We made the standard jokes about our penguin suits
It was one of those few times I realised
While it was happening, that my life was blessed,

And, as often, I was standing near someone
Who once had seen death leering from close up.

To say that sooner than listen to John Cage
You'd far rather listen to the Beach Boys
Is merely to register the difference
Between a footpath and a landslide

Cage has an apt last name, for he is locked
Up in there, at loggerheads with chaos.
And anyway, whatever made him think
That music was at an end?
It didn't even end when Little Richard
Sucked on a cake of soap.

Today and since it happened and far ahead,
Barber's Adagio for Strings
Is the music of 9/11
Nothing aleatoric about it: no dice were thrown
Just beauty, which at the end had better
Be anybody's fallback mode.

Last episode:
To my daughter's studio, and her portraits
Of my granddaughter growing.
And even just thinking of seeing this
In this most fruitful chapter of my life
I swear that I can hear the light
Rain through the leaves
While in my garden
The bowl of agapanthus

And the sprays of buddleia
Fight a battle of the purples,
An air-duel in the boudoir
Of the Lady Murasaki

*   *   *

This is my autumn's autumn. Claiming the use
Of so much splendour with my failing eyes
I take it as a sympathetic ruse
To glorify the path of one who dies
And see him out of the composing room,
The way the printers tapped out a farewell
For someone walking to a silent doom
After a life of noisy work done well
Among the old machines. So he moves on:
Othello, with his occupation gone.

He made that huge mistake about his wife
Because he listened to a chief of staff
Who saw no future in his master's life
That might include a decent battle. Laugh?
I tried to, as I left my main event,
Which was to write for print. Now, if I must,
Some bitching lyric about where time went
Is all I get done, a fate merely just
For someone drained of strength. This notebook here
Filled at the rate of forty lines a year.

But this much I can do. I can, with care,
Make every line count, and perhaps, some day,

Light on an argument that takes the air
As used to happen when I had my say
With ease. What once I could command at will,
The music of the syllables, has run
And hidden, but deep down I hear it still,
The same way I can see the autumn sun
Behind the screens of leaves, still shining through
As good as gold, as beautiful as you.

*   *   *

I had thought this ship was sailing
Across the river in the sky towards
Andromeda, but in the night, it stopped
Quite close to home, and on the quay
Boxes were swung ashore that indicated
Another destination altogether,
Somewhere nearby and just across the river.
Don't quiz me now on how I figured out
This was my destination, just a mile
Away, where my dear elder daughter
Had been building her new studio
Which I had longed to see, but in real life
Because too ill to move except at night
Though I had travelled many, many miles
I hadn't seen it. Now though, at long last
I could get into my wheelchair and across
The bridge into the park. My son-in-law
Had left to drive my granddaughter to school,
But everybody else was there to push me
And act as honour guard. Above the weir

The water was lit up and swans patrolled
As if a Fabergé shop window
Had been flown in to find a new Fontanka.
Students were playing soccer on the grass
Barefoot, a way, I could have told them,
To bust a toe and get an early look
At the new nurses in Addenbrooke's.

We got across the park into the maze
Of little streets that branch off the main road
And dawn had broken when they helped me
Out of the chair and into that small house
Which so far I had merely heard about
But only now could I begin to see
The splendour of, for everywhere on its two floors
Frames of white canvas being turned towards me
Revealed their colours, figures, forms and spaces
And some of them were of my granddaughter
Playing her violin, or even better
Searching it to pin down the right string
To stroke next so as to obtain the sound
She would need soon to polish off the phrase.
In every picture she wore different clothes –
They all must have been done at different times –
Yet here were steadily recurring themes
Of colour and of texture, those two things
Always related in such ways that light
Brought forth its shadows and each shadow, light:
The pastel slats and flats of light that build
A final darkness.

My elder daughter had a working day
Ahead of her. And so, too, did her mother
And her sister. High time, then, to wheel me home
Before they split up, and as we progressed
Adastrus spoke to me. "Remember, Caesar,
That you are mortal." Rather anomalous,
I thought, he being so non-Roman. Still,
He had the right idea. Back at the bridge
The swans had changed position, which is all
They ever do, as far as I can tell,
By way of dying. Maybe the same is true
For all of us. These were the years
I now see, that I became a part
Of my wife's scholarship, my elder daughter's
Painting, and her sister's deep enjoyment
Of all the best books about JFK.

I also featured, less than twenty-four
Hours ago, as an early customer
Of my granddaughter's new tea-shop,
Arranged in the front room of her house.
For medical reasons
I was not allowed to order anything
But I enjoyed the menu
When she read it out,
And there was some buttered bread
I was allowed to have,
And so she hovered there attentively
While I sat carefully not mentioning
I had been ill, and one day would be gone.

So full of fizzing pills that if you hit me
With a stick I would spill like a *piñata*
In a bon-bon shower of colours
I ride my wheelchair down the hill
To the festival with all of you as escort.
The footpaths are packed with families
With tots toted aloft on stronger shoulders
Than anything I've had to offer
For far too many years.
It is bonfire night, and if it were to prove
My last I don't see how I could complain.
The star-shells climb to gloriously burst
Spreading their splendour in a visual fanfare
That thrills me but can't give me strength.
Time to go home. My legs are cold.

I thought that I was vanishing, but instead
I was only coming true:
Turning to what, in seeming to end here,
Must soon continue
As the rain does the moment that it falls.